# BEYOND XEN

*"WHERE PASSION AND COMPASSION INTERSECT"*

ALEZIAH ELLIS

ISBN-13: 978-1539355717

L.O.C. - TXu002009522

# Acknowledgements

First and foremost, I give thanks, praise, and glory to my "Heavenly Father" who called and commissioned me to perfect His work.
To my Editor – Felicia Murrel, whose insightful and constructive professionalism proved paramount in leading me to the "first stage of the mountain," fellow Senior Author and mentor – Rick Knight, who further opened my eyes to the structured processes and unlimited possibilities of transforming from "Writer to Author," Richard Evans – book cover design Artist, and to all the other "Sherpa's" and influencer's who helped me bring this mountain top experience to life.

# Prologue

This book is an insightful representation of my personal "Faith Journey of Life" which has forced me to face an early childhood *epiphany moment* that occurred at the age of eight while growing up in Gary, Indiana – an industrial steel town in Northwest Indiana. While standing in a public library, as a very aspiring and forward thinking third grader, I told myself there would always be racism in America. But, I did not understand completely how I reached this conclusion. In spite of seeing and hearing about all of the historic racial progress (Laws/Policies/ Programs), works of great leaders from all walks of life, and even daring myself to dream that one day there would be a president of color in this great nation of ours, I still believed that the overall hatred that fueled our fears would continue to resonate above all and continue to restrict the way we live - today's *living testament*.

Since then, my journey has lead me on a life course through primary, secondary, and college education.

The family, corporate, spiritual, and social arenas have further shaped and molded my beliefs while equipping my mind and strengthening my courage to finally address this life-long challenge holistically with a different perspective, thus solidifying *my personal conviction of purpose*.

*"Within the depths of my soul – lies the true essence of my existence."*

*"To every man there comes in his lifetime that special moment; that moment, when he is figuratively tapped on the shoulder and offered a chance to do a very special thing, unique to him and fitted for his talents - What a tragedy, if that moment finds him unprepared, or unqualified, for the work which would be his finest hour." (Winston Churchill).*

*"There comes a time when one must take a position that is neither safe, nor politic, nor popular, but he must take it because conscience tells him it is right." (Dr. Martin Luther King, Jr.).*

• We must all develop the courage to follow Godly convictions and stop waiting on the world to change. Be the change you seek.

# A Message from the Author

## My Destiny Defined:

This Book helps to shine the light differently on people from all walks of life by elevating your consciousness of xenophobic delusion and liberating you from xenophobic practices that promote disunity.

- The goal of this book is to strip mankind down to flesh and bone, to a skinless state where indifference becomes invisible.

"For if any be a hearer of the word, and not a doer, he is like unto a man beholding his natural face in a mirror." (James 1:23).

"As long as race matters - there will always be confusion, delusion, and exclusion."

Proclamation: Speaks the truth in the face of collective delusion.

Please forward all inquiries to: aleziah17@gmail.com

This book is dedicated to all who believe in the power of the "Spirit" of change as well as to those who conform to the status quo of "waiting on the world to change."

I further dedicate this book to all mankind as the spirit himself has directed and guided me to tell this story as truthfully and honestly possible, for the betterment and advancement of cultural unity to all humanity of this generation and beyond.

This Book also serves as the cornerstone in promoting the "LifeWorkz Global Iniative" which is a non-profit 501(c)3 organization that is committed to bringing to life the principles set forth herein and 90% of all book sales proceeds shall be contributed to help support this cause.

Please feel free to visit us at: www.lifeworkzglo.org.

- *"Change never comes – It's created."*

# Contents

# Introduction

When we're all shipwrecked together stuck out in the middle of the sea, we tolerate each other. But, when we're rescued ashore, we retreat to *Xen* - Our isolated silos *of moral escape* where we are most comfortable practicing *xenophobic* works of darkness racism, distrust, hatred, exploitation, disrespect, insensitivity, discrimination, separatism, and other unnecessary iniquities. As believers, we are all members of the same Body of Christ, representing different parts whereby each is given certain spiritual *gifts* to be shared with one another collectively for the *common good.* Therefore, we should *all* endeavor to leave no one behind and move *Beyond Xen* – "Beyond the Darkness of Xenophobic Delusion."

## Theoretical references:

### Xenophobia
Intentionally harboring a phobic attitude and fear towards foreigners, strangers, unlike kinds, and the unknown while consciously practicing and promoting acts of degradation; hatred, racism, discrimination, segregation, etc.

### Delusion
Generally means mischaracterization of reality i.e. denial of the truth.

### Xenophobic Delusion
Xenophobic Delusion is the unabated denial of harboring a phobic attitude and fear towards foreigners, strangers, unlike kinds, and the unknown while consciously practicing and promoting acts of degradation exacted against others as it relates to our historic grievances regarding culture, slavery, poverty, inequality, racism, and segregation which cultivates and enforces our misguided existence of living.

- Xenophobia promotes a level of hatred so severe; it robs and blinds us from understanding that we need one another now more than ever to overcome the socioeconomic challenges of our time.

- Xenophobia destroys the very *fabric of our existence* and ruins our shared dominion on earth together as humans.

**XEN** *is comparable to that detestable food you refuse to eat unless you're starving.*

You can never discredit the truth because the truth never changes.

*Not seeing, yet believing is faith.*
*Seeing, yet not believing is delusion.*

## Racial Tolerance
Racial tolerance is a fair, objective, and permissive attitude toward those whose opinions, beliefs, practices, racial or ethnic origins, etc., differ from one's own; freedom from bigotry.

In society today, there normally exist only two stages in our life cycles when we find it totally acceptable to fully embrace one another as brothers and sisters in Christ:

- Infants – 5 years of age     and       Seniors 65 + (Racial Tolerance)

- 6 years of age     ----       64 years of age (Xenophobic Life)

## Racial Indifference
Racial indifference is a system of control that depends on the unconscious lack of compassion and caring about a minority race and  racial groups by purposely not extending the same recognition of  humanity and sympathy that is naturally extended to one's own group. It is fueled by unconscious racism.

When racial indifference is prevalent, people of various cultures assimilated within a given society, are like individual slices of assorted flavored cheesecake – vanilla, lemon, chocolate, almond, lime, orange, strawberry, etc. with various uniquely different toppings. At their core is the exact same basic ingredients down to the crust, but they tend to focus only on their surface differences.

*Hatred is taught – Love is learned*

## Inequality

Inequality is an unfair situation in which some groups in society have more money, opportunities, power etc. than others.

## Diversity

**The concept of diversity** encompasses **inclusion** and **respect**. It means understanding that each individual is unique, and recognizes our individual differences. These can be along the dimensions of race, ethnicity, gender, sexual orientation, socioeconomic status, age, physical abilities, religious beliefs, political beliefs, or other ideologies. It is the exploration of these differences in a safe, positive, and nurturing environment. It is about understanding each other and **moving beyond simple tolerance to embracing and celebrating the rich dimensions of diversity contained within each individual.**

## Believer's Preamble

Based on our current socioeconomic crisis, it is overwhelmingly apparent that America will be better served through serving one another, by casting aside all xenophobic fears. For if not, our livelihoods as we know them shall be irreversibly threatened.

*Xenophobia is considered the root and race is the victim.*

* Nothing lasts forever, not wealth, status, health, except that which God enables us to do for others - our good works.

*Getting what we don't deserve is* grace.
*Not getting what we deserve is* mercy.

## Religion

"We have just enough *religion* to make us hate, but not enough to make us love one another" (*Jonathan Swift*).

## Religion Parable:

Religious preferences can be compared to a supreme pizza with many toppings, i.e. the Body of Christ has many members. Everyone represents a slice of the same pizza and although they are the same size, shape, and form, we all become delusional about how we view our slices – my slice looks-smells-taste better. In essence, *my religion is superior to yours.*

- *Most believers only worship* **one God** *but idolize* **and serve many,** *both intentionally and unconsciously. These transitory gods are: self, celebrities, money, houses, cars, sex, drugs, alcohol, pets, etc.*

*"Although your house may be bigger than mine, our caskets will be the same size."*

# Liberation

Liberation is the act or process of freeing someone or something from another's control; the act of liberating someone or something. Liberation is also the act or fact of gaining equal rights or full social or economic opportunities for a particular group.

In order to be liberated from something, you have to be removed from it. It has to be eradicated. Since we're all enslaved by the misguided thoughts of our minds, believers in Christ have to learn to liberate their minds by *learning to live on the summit,* which is learning to live in the spirit versus living in the flesh (the abyss). "*Set your mind on things that are above, not on things that are on earth*" (colossians 3:2).

## *Deliverance*

Deliverance is a rescue from bondage or danger. A recovery or preservation from loss, but further entails a thought or judgment expressed; a formal or authoritative pronouncement.

A famous Rabbi while being interviewed by a top Business Executive, shared this spiritual truth,

"The Lord parts the Red Sea for many people daily, but most miss the signs."

*"Deliverance is a State of Mind – a Matter of Perspective."*

## *Freedom*

Freedom is the power or right to act, speak, or think as one wants without hindrance or restraint. Many governments, especially the United States, claim to guarantee freedom. But, often people do not, in fact, have the absolute freedom to act or speak without restraint.

*FREEDOM is not given – It's taken*

## *Goliath's of the World*

Injustices and indifferences are found among the Goliath's of the world's systems. They are: inequitable Political, Social, and Economic Systems, Poverty, Homelessness, Food Insecurity, Racial persecution, Economic Inequality, Mass Incarceration, Voter Suppression, Unjust Criminal Justice System, Separate & Unequal Schools, Racial, Class, and Religious Discrimination, and the like.

• To stand with Jesus is to have great skepticism about systems of power and a willingness to question the motives of the powerful. Or, as *James Baldwin* once penned to Angela Davis, "If we know, and do nothing, we are worse than the murderers hired in our name. If we know, then we must fight for your life as though it were our own— which it is—and render impassable with our bodies the corridor to the gas chamber. For, if they take you in the morning, they will be coming for us that night."

*"There's a Great Equalizer of the Universe who always balances the Scale."*

# Chapter 1
# A Nation is Born

*A nation is a large aggregate of people united by common descent, history, culture, or language, inhabiting a particular country or territory that is sufficiently conscious of its unity to seek or to possess a government peculiarly to its own and that is controlled by its own government.*

**BEGINNING WITH THE REVOLUTIONARY WAR** whereby we gained our freedom from British tyranny in 1776, America was born and built on illusionary religious principles and her competitive advantage has always been her *exceptionalism* – our rights, our freedoms, our values. Today, it is rapidly eroding at its core. Our Pledge of Allegiance – One Nation Under God, Indivisible with Liberty and Justice for All, U.S. Creeds such as; Land of The Free, Home of The Brave, United We Stand, etc. are being reduced to nothing more than national *propaganda*. Our government has failed consistently over the last 150 years in its frugal attempt to devise *Equal and Social Rights* policies that protect and ensure equal rights for all U.S. citizens. Though, measurable gains have been made with passing two of the most significant laws of the nineteenth and twentieth century's– the *13th* Amendment *to the U.S. Constitution in 1865,* which on its surface, officially ended slavery as we knew it, even though slavery continued illegally throughout the deep south for the next fifty years and the Civil Rights Act of 1964 which outlawed discrimination based on race, color, religion, sex or national origin and officially made segregation in public facilities illegal. Even today, minorities' have yet to be openly welcomed, nor receive equal treatment, nor have equal economic opportunities been afforded to them overall. Additionally, with the enactment of the *Voter's Rights Act of 1965* which prohibited racial discrimination in voting and is viewed by the U.S. Department of Justice as the single most important legislation ever passed in this country, this law has been vigorously challenged and voter fraud and suppression continues today. Furthermore, in *1962,* the U.S. Supreme Court passed a law that declared prayer *in public schools as unconstitutional* via *Separation of State and Religion* which began an unofficial anti-religious movement that influenced further removal of prayer and religious scripture from all public places to include specifically courthouses and most other public facilities nationwide, thus censoring religion out of public view. In1973, with the legalizing of abortions, the U.S. continued to stray further away from religious beliefs. This has resulted in excess of 53 million abortions in the U.S. since 1973. Furthermore, the Supreme Court ruled in *1980* that the posting of the Ten Commandments was equally unconstitutional in public schools and buildings. In addition, July 2015, the Supreme Court legalized gay marriage in all fifty States which sparked much controversy. These laws and practices have fueled a constant decline of national religious values by creating a moresecular nation and severely eroding national *morality.*

## Liberty and Justice for All ...except?

The founding principles of the United States of America being **Liberty and Justice for all are more theoretical than practical.** European Americans are here because of blood, and mostly that of others; here because of their insatiable and rapacious desire to take by force the land and labor of those others by any means necessary. Immediately following our triumph in the Revolutionary War, our founding principles have only applied to White citizens of this nation. Native Americans and Negroes were presumably excluded from this newly gained "Liberty and Justice for All." Native Americans were stripped, forced, and defrauded out of their land and livelihoods. Negroes, were forcibly kidnapped and casted into slavery while America was under British rule (1607 – 1776), they were never conceived to be protected under these new founding principles. After U.S. Independence, the majority of Native Americans were either killed in battle, starved due to the annihilation of their main food supply (Buffaloes were slaughtered en masse), or they died from the small pox disease contracted from Europeans. Negroes, on the other hand, remained physically enslaved until 1865, when slavery officially ended with the North's Civil War victory and the enactment of the thirteenth Amendment, however they have remained socially and politically enslaved ever since.

# The Great U.S. Economic War

The entire U.S. economy was built on slavery and the institution of slavery was its absolute most prosperous business enterprise for 246 official years (1619 – 1865), though the practice continued well into the 1920's.

In 1860, prior to the commencement of the Great Civil War, the Confederate Southern States were a powerful and independent nation whose total economy was built on cotton, tobacco, and rice production based on African slave labor.
There were an estimated 3.96 million slaves throughout the South. Collectively, they generated a total gross domestic product (GDP) estimated at $4 billion, which valued their economy as the fourth richest country worldwide.

The original thirteen colonies also built their independent colonies from slave labor, but somewhat different in nature, five out of thirteen colonies were southern. Slavery was legal and practiced in each of the thirteen colonies. In most places, it involved house servants or farm workers. It was of more economic importance in the export-oriented tobacco plantations of Virginia and Maryland, rice and indigo plantations of South Carolina, and cotton in Georgia. About 100,000 slaves were imported into the eight Northern colonies with estimated economic value in 1860 of about $300 million (Virginia, North Carolina, South Carolina, and Georgia are captured in the Confederate Southern States GDP estimates referenced above). Maryland, although classified as Southern, was not a member of the Confederacy and therefore operated as a somewhat wildcard colony that controlled about 88,000 slaves that generated an economic windfall of about $264 million.

- The Northern colonies, although they benefited less from direct slavery labor profits, struck gold in financing 90% of the total slave trade business. Most of the wealthiest bankers and financiers resided in New York where slave trade investing was the single most lucrative, risk-free investment worldwide.

## A Nation United by War

The last time this country of ours faced such a defining moment as today, was not1964, with the passing of the then historic Civil Rights Act, but was from 1861 -1865; the Civil or Economic War. In 1863, President Lincoln signed into law the ***Emancipation Proclamation*** granting freedom to all Negro slaves and also granting them the right to enlist in the Union Army, which became one of the most courageous and defining moments in our country's dynamic history. Although President Lincoln contemplated this historic decision for over a year, his leadership and foresight prevailed due to him understanding that one of the most important ***purposes of the war was to end the institution of slavery*** which had singlehandedly divided this great country. President Lincoln also knew the war could not be won without allowing every able body Negro citizen or slave the right to enlist in the Union Army and join in the fight for their freedom. His decisive actions demanded great courage and diplomacy due to the fact that the entire Union Army, Congress and most Yankee citizens were deeply opposed to such action. He persuaded them all that it was in the best interest of moving the country forward, and not only was the war a decisive victory for him, it proved to be the right decision as history has confirmed. He knowingly understood that the war was soon ending, victory was imminent, and he passionately proceeded to gain support in garnering a consensus in the House to agree to pass the thirteenth amendment of the Constitution. The Senate had previously passed the bill on April 8, 1864, which in its literal composition abolished slavery permanently and granted equal rights to all citizens – to include Negroes and all other minorities for the first time in our nations' history, prior to the end of the war. President Lincoln being a lawyer by training and a prophet by grace, understood the fact that the 1863 Emancipation Proclamation was a temporary document that he alone executed as commander-in-chief with war power authority and that in order to remain enforceable after the war, the Constitution would have to be amended. He further knew that under current State laws regarding slavery, each Southern state regarded slaves as real property and that unless the U.S. Constitution was amended prior to the end of the war, there would be no legal ground for the Federal government to prevent these Southern states from continuing slavery because the slave owners under State protected property rights would be allowed to do as they please with their own personal property. After much persuasion and intense negotiations, the House finally passed the Bill on ***January 31, 1865.*** The Civil War ended thereafter on ***March 4, 1865***.

• Unfortunately, a little more than a month later, on April 15, 1865, President Lincoln was assassinated mainly due to his firm convictions of equality for all people.

## *Main Driving Force of Lincoln's Conviction of Equality:*
Lincoln displayed little doubt that it was God that controls man's destiny, not man. He wrestled with the notion of whether we are fitted to the times we are born into.

He studied and nearly mastered the Six-books of Euclid - *Euclid's Elements*, Published 300 B.C.), which he embraced wholeheartedly being convinced that – "Things that are equal to the same thing are equal to one another;" which became his foundational basis for promoting human equality.

• President Lincoln was fitted above and beyond his time.

"There's a great invisible strength in a peoples' union."
                                          - President Lincoln

## Peonage

Beginning in 1874, just nine short years after the ending of the Civil War, White southern elites were left with desolate lands and severe income losses which prompted them to employ a system of Peonage (Indentured Servitude) targeting formerly freed Black slaves. As a result, thousands of black men and teenage males were illegally convicted of petty crimes that resulted in extended prison sentences for the purpose of bringing rise to a "Convict Leasing Program" whereby these convicts were leased by the respective Southern States to individual land owners and Companies for profit – fueling a multi-million dollar Industrial revolution throughout the South. Birmingham, Alabama was the number one benefactor whereby such labor fueled their massive Steel production, while other Southern States built railroads, produced agriculture, and clay bricks for construction. This practice proved to be even more profitable than slavery; slaves were more expensive to purchase usually ranging from $500 - $2,000 each, and were therefore protected by their respective owners for a lifetime investment that extended across several generations through breeding offspring to repeat this cycle. On the other hand, "Convicts" were leased by respective states on the average of $9.00 per month to various private corporations or individual land owners. Often times, they were sold directly to private investors who eagerly purchased the legal fee debts from the respective State Courts when state prisons became extensively overcrowded. This new form of negro labor was not only cheaper to acquire than traditional slaves, but also less expensive to replace and maintain.

## The Great Migration

These unjust and illegal persecutions resulting from the "Peonage System," directly fueled a "New Movement". "**The Great Negro Migration**" was born **(1915 – 1970)** whereby six million plus Southern Negroes collectively participated in a mass exodus out of Southern States resettling in specific industrial Midwestern and Northern states and certain Western agricultural states respectively to escape these harsh conditions. To date, this represents the most extensive migratory movement to ever occur in the U.S.A. and is responsible for fueling the "Industrial Revolution" that created millions of new jobs throughout the country, specifically in the cities of Chicago, Illinois; Detroit, Michigan; Gary, Indiana; Youngstown, Ohio; New York, New York; Pittsburgh, Pennsylvania; and Los Angeles and Oakland, California, respectively.

In spite of the major contributions that Negroes made in creating the agricultural and infrastructure development which laid the foundation for the nation's sustainability and growth, they were relegated to being invisible U.S. casualties. What is even more disturbing is that these same founding principles were based largely from God's principles of righteous spiritual living. Whose God? Clearly, there exist blatant collective delusion.

## *Case in Point:*
*America's Delusion of Slavery – Sugarcoating the Truth*

In spite of all of the deplorable U.S. history of slavery and its ensuing dehumanizing persecutions, still today, America remains in denial.

A recent October 2015 incident exposed by a fifteen year old Pearland, Texas High School Student – Coby Burrenan, an African American male who became infuriated when he saw a map caption in his World Geography Textbook (section – *"Patterns of Immigration"*) that depicted the following: The Atlantic Slave Trade from 1500 – 1800 brought millions of "Workers from Africa" to the southern U.S. to work on "Agricultural Plantations" – giving the indication that this was voluntary immigration versus forced slavery.

He became so upset, that he sent a text of the caption to his mother, a University of Houston Doctoral student who upon receipt, immediately contacted McGraw-Hill Education (world'stenth largest educational book Publisher). McGraw-Hill immediately acknowledged the mistake and apologized while further agreeing to distribute revised textbooks with "stickers" to correct the inaccurate caption. This is not the first time that McGraw-Hill Education has been caught with their hand in the cookie jar in Texas; since 2010, McGraw-Hill along with several other national publishers have been cited for several other Texas textbooks that were ultimately deemed inaccurate, biased, and politicized, yet still approved by the Texas Board of Education.

A total of 150,000 of these erroneous textbooks had already been distributed to other Texas High school students which created a major challenge to correct. Furthermore, Texas has a great influence over the content of all U.S. Public School textbooks and the teaching of history because it is one of the nation's largest textbook purchasing markets (Texas *has 5.2 million K – 12 Public School Students*) and regularly serves as the "National Beta Test" for the entire nation for all new text book releases. Once new textbooks have been published that meet Texas standards, they are distributed throughout other states.

Although band-aid corrections were made in Texas, there still exists hundreds of thousands or more of these same "tarnished" textbooks that have already been distributed throughout the nation which causes one to wonder if – McGraw-Hill has the integrity to voluntarily correct them as well or will they simply just sit back and wait to be notified respectively? Myself being a first-time Author, and understanding how exhaustive and meticulous the process of composing a good book of any kind can be, find it hard to believe that this is simply an error that neither the Author, nor Editor, nor Publisher, nor Texas School Administrators caught? To date, no one at McGraw-Hill has taken direct responsibility for this "gross misrepresentation of the truth."

*The U.S. was built on slavery and its offspring is racism.*

## The American Dream

**According to excerpts from a recent 2015 Brooking Report Study**, *OPPORTUNITY, RESPONSIBILITY, and SECURITY: A CONSENSUS PLAN FOR REDUCING POVERTY AND RESTORING THE AMERICAN DREAM:*

In 1931, the writer James Truslow Adams coined the term The American Dream. His definition holds up well today. The dream, he said, is of a land in which, "life should be better and richer and fuller for everyone, with opportunity for each according to ability or achievement."

It is a difficult dream for the European upper class to interpret adequately, and too many of us ourselves have grown weary and mistrustful of it.

It is not a dream of material wealth and high wages merely, but a dream of social order in which each man and each woman shall be able to attain to the fullest stature of which they are capable, and be recognized by others for what they are, regardless of the fortuitous circumstances of birth or position.

Today, many Americans fear that our country is no longer a land of opportunity. Social mobility (a person's movement over time from one class to another, which can be up or down) overall seems to have decreased in recent decades;

- There is evidence that social mobility is lower in America than in any other advanced economies.

The reasons for the increasing gaps between childhoods in different social classes, while many, are often intertwined. These include: the loss of manufacturing jobs, stagnating wages for workers without a college degree, labor-saving technological changes, changing relationships between workers and management, the increasing importance of education and training in a post-industrial economy, a less energetic civil society, disproportionately high rates of incarceration, weaker attachment to the labor force among less-educated men, and the rising prevalence of single-parent families among the less-educated.

The poor prospects for children born into poor families are an urgent national concern. This state of affairs contradicts our country's founding ideals.

> The massive waste and loss of this human potential costs the United States $500 billion annually in economic terms, and it is a tragedy in human terms. Most Americans would agree that we have to do better.

> *"The American dream is like a greyhound dog race. The dogs all win various races, but never catch the golden rabbit of economic freedom."*

## America - The Xenophobic Society

Currently in the U.S. today, we all live in a Xenophobic Society. This is a term typically used to denote a phobic attitude and fear towards foreigners or strangers, or even of the unknown. Racism in general is described as a form of **xenophobia** as it relates to our historic grievances regarding culture, slavery, poverty, inequality, racism, and segregation which cultivates and enforces our misguided existence of living in **isolated silos** politically/culturally/religiously/socially which has created two distinctive separate and unequal societies. As a result, racial relations are worse today than they have been since the Civil War ended in 1865. Politicians, religious leaders, social scientists, and White citizens tend to boast about all of the significant progress that has been made in racial equality in regards to African Americans and other minorities, citing more specifically the Civil Rights Act of 1964, Affirmative Action Programs, Social Entitlement Programs, Minority Business Set-A-Side Programs, Corporate Diversity Programs, and other minority based laws and initiatives. While all of these initiatives have proven to be successful in *pacifying* the racial, cultural, and economic divide between White and Black America, they remain only metaphoric ***truths*** of denial of the facts of today- separate and unequal. It is actually assumed by our conservatively liberal society that the race **issue** is a half **dormant**, but easily awakened **beast.** However, by agreeing to restrict the consideration of race and racism (defined as racial indifference), daily *life can remain comfortable for those in the morally corrupt Xenophobic Society.*

- *"Fences, walls, and systems are incapable of protecting us from the enemy within. You can't hide from yourself because everywhere you go, there you are."*

The vast majority of social **scientists** are prisoners of their own times and have historically proven to be incapable of answering ethical, moral, and religious questions. *It takes a person with a new vision* to break with the prejudices of these times…UNSEEN – UNKNOWN – UNIMAGINED.

*A Sherpa for higher truths in these times of crisis – one of the chosen few of us "fitted above and beyond our time."*

## Enslaved by the Misguided Thoughts of Our Minds

Although we promote the U.S.A as land of the free and the home of the brave, how can we be free or brave if we are *all living in fear* (xenophobia*)? For anything that overcomes you, enslaves you.*

We live in two separate societies within this country —separate and unequal. We fear ourselves and one another which has resulted in increased segregation and inequality that is far more damaging today than at any other time in our history. We all live in *communal silos* that provide us with a false sense of security – politically, culturally, religiously, and socially. *Galatians 3:28* instructs us that "There is neither Jew nor Greek nor slave nor free, for we are all one in Jesus Christ Lord of All." Considering that the majority of the U.S. population proclaim to be self-professed **believers in Christ,** why have sisterly/brotherly/neighborly love not been holistically practiced by so called Christians as a whole beyond race, class, and quotas? Obviously prejudice, discrimination, segregation, racial violence, and unjustifiable hatred practices take precedence over righteousness. Xenophobic practices are sinful acts that unmistakably enslave us.

*The fear of anything can produce physical symptoms of it.*

*We have only one thing together on this Earth, dominion. We are all sharing this world together. We don't own the world. We're not kings here, nor are we God. And when we become selfish, it fuels our desire for control which leads us to tempt ourselves into believing we are a god. It's just a sinful illusion.*

- History has taught us that laws, policies, and procedures are deemed ineffective in influencing compassionate **change of heart** in the minds of the power structure.

# Chapter 2

# A Nation Divided
# Shall Never Prosper

*The **United States of America** although "**United**" by state territories - remains divided socially, politically, and religiously, due to her historical illusion of fostering sovereign democracy and unity.*

*"Every kingdom divided against itself will be laid waste, and every city or household divided against itself will not stand."*
*(Matthew 12:25).*

**IN TERMS OF SOCIAL REFORM** as a country, we are clearly moving in reverse instead of forward. Although we have made great strides as the result of the historic Civil Rights Act of 1964 and Voters Right of 1965, today, the U.S.A is more divided than any other time in history – *separate* and *unequal*.

As recent as June 24, 2013, the Supreme Court ruled 5 – 4, to strike down the heart of the Voters Rights Act of 1965 by freeing nine States (mostly Southern: Alabama, Alaska, Arizona, Georgia, Louisiana, Mississippi, South Carolina, Texas and Virginia) to change their election laws without Federal approval due largely in part to fifty-year old outdated coverage formulas that no longer apply. Critics, along with Chief Justice Roberts, suggested that racial discrimination protection was no longer needed in these respective states and that the election of our country's first Black president, Barak Obama is a resounding confirmation. As a result, all of these respective States have begun to implement new voting policies, first tested in the November 2014 midterm elections that are more restrictive and suppressive towards minorities. The results were questionable and several Voter Suppression lawsuits were filed challenging voting validity in many of these newly exempted States.

Ironically, the single most segregated institutions in the U.S. today are churches and houses of worship, whereby most are consistently segregated by race and the shameful practice of xenophobic delusion is more subtle to say the least. Even the few churches that are so called interdenominational with varied diversity of race and cultures, still lack fundamental **cultural unity.** At most, it appears to be just more window dressing. We see churches around the country where God only shows up to an isolated few, but quickly leaves their circle in search of more spiritual houses. Where is the house where God and man can show up at the same time and the same place? *Bethany House – a place for revival where God finds a resting place on earth.* Most church's today, are not prepared for a "Revival," because they are not spiritually prepared for the manifest presence of God.

- *Bethany* is a small town located about 1.5 miles east of Jerusalem and has traditionally been identified with the present-day West Bank city of al-Eizariya (Arabic (العيزرية), meaning "*Place of Lazarus*"),;

- *Bethany* (translated): House of mourning and poverty – a place of revival. It represented a rare spiritual atmosphere that made it comfortable and appealing to Christ because care for the poor is a sacred duty and concern of God's own heart.

*Because Jesus was "dual natured*," he had to find a place where he could be hosted as man and equally worshipped for divinity at the same time; a place of hospitality (*Martha*) and a place of worship for divinity (*Mary*)…"**House of Bethany.**"

"The church must become spiritually ambidextrous if it hopes to do the work of God which requires us to be so credible and compassionate in the human realm that we can say, "Come meet somebody," and the people in the community will listen and come. The church must be so passionate in the spiritual realm that we say, "Lord, come meet somebody," and He will be proud to take his seat in the throne of our praise" (Tommy Tenney).

- Religion should be more about spiritual relationship than spiritual division.

The dark shadow of slavery still permeates today, casting itself over every aspect of American life.

## The Rise of Civil Disobedience

Additionally, with all of the recent increase of police violence shootings of minority citizens nationwide, civil unrest in the twenty-first century is at a near crisis **point.** Civil liberties have dramatically eroded.

As a result, civil disobedience has now escalated into a more commonly employed moral weapon in the fight for justice. ***"Unjust laws are like no laws at All"*** (St. Augustine). The current majority has consistently pleaded the fifth and chosen moral escape versus justice for all. Hiding in darkness will never shield you from the light.

Violence against U.S. citizens of color is at an all-time high with police brutality escalating more frequently into suspicious deaths, unjust incarcerations, and unnecessary harassment. The recent wave of countless unjustifiable deaths of minorities, especially young black men and women by police and private white citizens have set off a firestorm of civil unrest unseen since the 1960's – 1970's. New 2015 social science studies are now concluding that the level of fear minorities, especially blacks in the U.S. face today may be associated with causing Post Traumatic Stress Disorder (PTSD) which historically had been reserved only for military war veterans. This new phenomenon has resulted from 400 plus years of slavery plus a culmination of all the racial hatred waged against blacks and other minorities to date, self-evident of our xenophobic society. The evidence is so relevant that most blacks of all ages and classes live in fear of racial attack and those with young children are being counseled on how to prevent their children and themselves from becoming victims of police violence while whites continue to live their normal lives, comfortably tucked away in their communal silos as always. Minorities, specifically black people, are not interested in having more unproductive conversations regarding race. They understand that law enforcement alone is not the problem. They are only manifestations of the larger xenophobic society that harbors the fears and hatred of indifference against people of color.

When the protection of human laws has been withdrawn from those who honor God, there will be in different lands, a *simultaneous movement* for their destruction. We see this trending now. As a result, many new activist groups have emerged to include Black Lives Matter (International Voice of Minorities of Color) which has held various marches, rallies, sit-ins, social media campaigns, and other demonstrations. Their movement has become so effective that the US Government's Homeland Security has unfairly labeled them as a terrorist group. Seemingly, a counter White activist group (All Lives Matter) was formed specifically as a direct rebuttal to denounce the views and opinions of Black Lives Matter, and mind you Homeland Security does not classify them as a terrorist threat, further solidifying the racial divide of separate and unequal.

- Ironically, simultaneous movements are playing out internationally and more specifically throughout all of Western civilization where capitalism is king and European culture has dominated and oppressed its disenfranchised minority brethren for centuries through imposing multitudes of biased socioeconomic systems, laws, and policies that restrict upward mobility and diminish future aspirations.

- "It does not belong to man…to direct his step" (Jeremiah 10:23) – Man historically has failed at setting moral standards.

## Age of Minority College Students Activism

Minority students enrolled at predominately White universities nationwide have consistently been exposed to various forms of racism ever since these respective schools became integrated, however today such students have a bigger voice. Due to the advancement of social media and similar electronic technologies, students now have a larger, broader, and more connected audience in which to vent their displeasures. This new social arena tends to expose the darkness of xenophobic practices carried out by the insensitive White majority and thus casts a negative perception about the entire university.

- A major part of this trending challenge, centers on the definition **of diversity** versus the practice **of diversity.**

This very issue is playing out across all spectrums of American society and the challenges are the same.

Most can agree on the defined meaning of diversity. It means understanding that each individual is unique, and recognizing our individual differences. These can be along the dimensions of race, ethnicity, gender, sexual orientation, socioeconomic status, age, physical abilities, religious beliefs, political beliefs, or other ideologies and encompasses acceptance, inclusion, and respect. But the practice of diversity rarely embraces acceptance, inclusion, and respect. Most public and private institutions tend to view diversity as nothing more than a twenty-first century Affirmative Action program of Color Coding, and THEREIN LIES THE PROBLEM.

## *Cases in Point:*

In response to recent racial tensions rising at the University of Missouri and Yale University, the following insight is provided in a recent 2015, *Atlanta Journal Constitution (AJC)* Article – "Get Schooled" by Maureen Downey

- Two universities have been roiled by alleged racist incidents that students of color say speak to a larger problem of racism on the campuses and in the culture.

On November 9, 2015, the University of Missouri president stepped down in response to mounting pressure, including the football team's refusal to play while he remained in office (which would have cost the School about $1 million to forfeit the game) and the student government's demand for his resignation. Critics said President Tim Wolfe ignored or downplayed racism on the Columbia, Missouri, campus and was slow to respond to the growing outrage of students and faculty.

Minority students have been citing overt acts of racism at the Missouri flagship. The president of the students' association reported two occasions when racial slurs were screamed at him. When Missouri Students Association President Payton Head shared those moments online in September, the floodgates opened and others shared their experiences.

- "I really just want to know why my simple existence is such a threat to society," Head wrote, "for those of you who wonder why I'm always talking about the importance of inclusion and respect, it's because I've experienced moments like this multiple times at THIS University, making me not feel included here."

- In his post, Head mentioned aggression against a Muslim woman who wears the hijab, a transgender student who was spat on downtown and students with disabilities trying to navigate Memorial Union. He talked about women who feel uncomfortable walking outside at night. In both the post and the interview, he described his experience walking past a bar with his partner and having drinks thrown at them.

- Cynthia Frisby, an associate professor in the Missouri School of Journalism wrote on Facebook about her own experiences with racism, "My most recent experience was while jogging on Route K in May 2015, when I was approached by a White man in a White truck with a Confederate flag very visible and proudly displayed. He leaned out his window (now, keep in mind I run against traffic, so his behavior was a blatant sign that something was about to happen). Not only did he spit at me, he called me the n-word and gave me the finger.

In New Haven, Connecticut, Yale University is grappling with student accounts of overt racist acts, some related to social settings.

- In one alleged incident, disputed by fraternity leaders, a student says women of color were rebuffed from entering a Sigma Alpha Epsilon party by someone saying the event was White girls only.

That incident led other students to contend the Ivy League campus is unaware or unconcerned with the challenges underrepresented minorities face. A series of protests led Yale President Peter Salovey to meet with students to discuss their experiences. His response as a result of that meeting, "I would say that to have about fifty minority students in a room with me saying to me that their experience was not what they hoped it would be, I take personal responsibility for that and I consider it a failure."

Here is an excerpt by Rachel Wilkinson, an African American Senior at Yale on her personal experience at Yale:

- "My status as a Yale student hasn't protected me from racist behavior on this campus, and my Yale degree won't protect me from racism in whatever office I work in or neighborhood I live in after graduation. One of the most important lessons I learned in my time at Yale is that systems of oppression are ubiquitous, and that no combination of good intentions and advanced education will ever make someone immune from the tendency to perpetuate racial biases. As author Junot Díaz once said, "White supremacy's greatest trick is that it has convinced people that it exists always in other people, never in us.""

Unfortunately, racism in and of itself is delusional. It has been positioned as only a belief system and not a powe rstruggle. Racism is a system of advantage based on race. The system is designed to make one believe that if you just act right, you'll reach the safety of rarified air. Then they remind you not to breathe. The majority of minorities are left feeling like they don't own their humanity. Achievements and accomplishments by minorities are not a shield against racism.

- Just as in 1776, when America won her independence from British rule, Native Americans and Negroes were relegated to being invisible U.S. casualties, in regards to citizenship rights, which was repeated in 1865, at the end of the Civil War. Though the official institution of slavery ended, Negroes and other minorities remained invisible citizens in the eyes of the moral majority. Sadly, in 2015, the saga of exclusionism and racism continue.

Furthermore, the newly trending Stand-Your-Ground law that has been enacted in twenty-three States, authorizes every citizen the right to not retreat from a threatening situation and use deadly force to defend themselves in any place or time. Also trending is the *Open-Carry* law. This law has been enacted by fifteen states and authorizes citizens to openly carry firearms as long as they are registered. The results of these new firearm laws have led to disproportionate increases in homicide rates and are fueling racial bias in law enforcement and private citizens alike. Also, the number of firearms sold to American customers has reached an all-time high with total U.S. *gun sales in 2011 at 6.2 million and 8.3 million in 2012, a 35% increase.* While White males comprise only one-third of the U.S. population, they represent 60% of gun ownership and the U.S. ranks number one worldwide in civilian gun ownership. Although the U.S. only represents 5% of the world's population, it is home to 35-50% of the world's civilian owned guns... xenophobia personified.

## Rampant Daily Mass Shootings in the U.S.

According to a recent article published in *Think Progress*, by Alan Pyke, there have been 355 mass shootings this year in the United States, more than one for every day of the year so far.

- In fact, the United States is the world leader when it comes to mass shootings. Despite having 5% of the world's population, the U.S. is home to 31% of the world's mass shootings since 1966.

A number of factors contribute to this, but the high rate of gun ownership seems to play a key role. In fact, the connection between gun ownership rates and mass shooting rates isn't unique to the U.S. which ranks number one worldwide in gun ownership per capita, followed by Finland and Switzerland, respectively.

In contrast, countries like Australia and Great Britain have done much to rein in gun ownership and mass shootings in turn. In Australia, efforts like buyback programs, extended waiting periods for gun purchases (measured in weeks, not days), a national firearms registry, limits on ammunition, and bans on many semi-automatic, self-loading rifles, and shotguns have made a huge difference. The country has had very few mass shootings since these changes were implemented in 1996 and the changes also contribute to a decline in the firearm homicide rate by 59% and a decline in the firearm suicide rate by 65%, with no corresponding non-firearm increases in either.

- In America, we are truly delusional if we believe that our xenophobic practices of gun violence are the answer to solving our historical racial differences. We must all learn to unite in Christ and reconcile our differences.

# The Powerful influence of the National Rifle Association (NRA)

A recent article published in *Think Progress* by Alex Zielinski disclosed the far-reaching influence the NRA has not only in Washington, but on the entire Medical Industry alike.

Mass shootings, gang violence, domestic abuse, suicide, accidents — gun violence in the United States comes in many forms. In the past week, the country has seen already two mass shootings. Every day, eighty-nine people die because of gun-related violence. Experts estimate guns may soon surpass vehicle accidents to the country's leading cause of deaths. President Barack Obama has repeatedly urged lawmakers to not make this the new normal.

But when it comes to finding solutions to this national problem, there's a major roadblock standing in the way. It's been decades since any federally-funded scientific research has been done on the issue.

That's why members of Congress joined physicians from across the country Wednesday morning to demand an end to the Dickey Amendment, a twenty-year-old law banning any scientific research on gun violence.

"Gun violence is among the most difficult public health challenges we face as a country, but because of the deeply misguided ban on research, we know very little about it," said Rep. David Price, vice chair to the House of Representatives' Gun Violence Prevention Task Force. Regardless of where we stand in the debate over gun violence, we should all be able to agree that this debate should be informed by objective data and robust scientific research.

## *On public health matters, it's critical we listen to Doctors—not Politicians.*

This ban, supported by the National Rifle Association (NRA), has effectively silenced researchers at both the Center for Disease Control and Prevention (CDC) and National Institute of Health (NIH) from conducting any comprehensive studies on what causes violence — and what can be done to prevent it — since 1996. As expected, it's left public health experts and policymakers with little to lean on as they attempt to craft new legislation to help quell the fatal trend.

- On Wednesday, December 2, 2015, a press conference led by Doctors for America, doctors presented a petition signed by more than 2,000 physicians in all fifty states requesting an end to the restriction.

"It's disappointing to me that we've made little progress in the past twenty years in finding solutions to gun violence," said Dr. Nina Agrawal, who's been a pediatrician in the South Bronx for years. "In my career, I've seen children's lives saved from measles, Sudden Infant Death Syndrome, motor vehicle accidents.because of federal scientific data and research. It's frustrating that the CDC is not permitted to do the same type of research for gun violence."

Instead, GOP leaders have tried to make gun violence an issue that requires mental health research, despite the fact that less than 3% of U.S. crimes involve someone with a mental illness. And the most recent argument against CDC funded research is that a gun is not a disease, even though the CDC has been researching motor vehicles, natural disasters, poor ventilation systems, and many other topics that wouldn't be labeled a disease for years. The politicians behind these arguments have yet to suggest allocating money to another government agency.

"Politicians have put a gag order on public health research for gun violence only to score political points," said Rep. Carolyn Maloney, who also spoke at the event. "On public health matters, it's critical we listen to doctors — not politicians."

**Common sense dictates we need to do something about this.**

Some have tried to roll back these restrictions before. In 2012, following the Newtown, Connecticut, school shooting, President Barack Obama signed an executive order to restore funds to gun violence studies.

- **Congress** has consistently blocked the initial amendment, though the law itself remains in place. Even the congressman who lent his name to the initial amendment, former Rep. Jay Dickey, has publicly expressed his regret for backing the bill.

"Using emotions and belief systems to address policy is a bad idea and is going to get us nowhere. So to develop effective policy we must conduct evidence-based research," said Dr. David Berman, a physician from St. Petersburg, Florida, who spoke. "**Common sense dictates we need to do something about this**."

Out of frustration with Congress' continuous support of the NRA and its refusal to address the deplorable gun violence crisis in the U.S., President Barack Obama signed an Executive Action on Gun Safety on January 5, 2016, making it harder to purchase guns in the U.S. A total of twenty-three Executive Order initiatives were signed into law as follows:

## Gun Violence Reduction Executive Actions:

1. Issue a Presidential Memorandum to require federal agencies to make relevant data available to the federal background check system.

2. Address unnecessary legal barriers, particularly relating to the Health Insurance Portability and Accountability Act that may prevent states from making information available to the background check system.

3. Improve incentives for states to share information with the background check system.

4. Direct the Attorney General to review categories of individuals prohibited from having a gun to make sure dangerous people are not slipping through the cracks.

5. Propose rulemaking to give law enforcement the ability to run a full background check on an individual before returning a seized gun.

6. Publish a letter from Bureau of Alcohol, Tobacco, Firearms and Explosives (ATF) to federally licensed gun dealers providing guidance on how to run background checks for private sellers.

7. Launch a national safe and responsible gun ownership campaign.

8. Review safety standards for gun locks and gun safes (Consumer Product Safety Commission).

9. Issue a Presidential Memorandum to require federal law enforcement to trace guns recovered in criminal investigations.

10. Release a Department of Justice (DOJ) report analyzing information on lost and stolen guns and make it widely available to law enforcement.

11. Nominate an ATF director.

12. Provide law enforcement, first responders, and school officials with proper training for active shooter situations.

13. Maximize enforcement efforts to prevent gun violence and prosecute gun crime.

14. Issue a Presidential Memorandum directing the Center for Disease Control to research the causes and prevention of gun violence.

15. Direct the Attorney General to issue a report on the availability and most effective use of new gun safety technologies and challenge the private sector to develop innovative technologies.

16. Clarify that the Affordable Care Act does not prohibit doctors asking their patients about guns in their homes.

17. Release a letter to health care providers clarifying that no federal law prohibits them from reporting threats of violence to law enforcement authorities.

18. Provide incentives for schools to hire school resource officers.

19. Develop model emergency response plans for schools, houses of worship and institutions of higher education.

20. Release a letter to state health officials clarifying the scope of mental health services that Medicaid plans must cover.

21. Finalize regulations clarifying essential health benefits and parity requirements within ACA exchanges.

22. Commit to finalizing mental health parity regulations.

23. Launch a national dialogue led by Secretaries Sebelius and Duncan on mental health.

It does not appear that *any* of the executive orders would have any impact on the guns people currently own or would like to purchase. And, all proposals regarding limiting the availability of assault weapons or large ammunition magazines will be proposed for Congressional action.

- Despite the fact that less than 3% of U.S. crimes involves someone with a mental illness, President Obama's Executive Orders place much emphasis on Mental Health Evaluations, but failed to address The most restrictive legal barrier to conducting hard scientific research is the Dickey Amendment, which for the last twenty years continues to ban all levels of medical research on gun violence. Even though Congress has demonstrated overwhelmingly in favor of eliminating this restrictive Amendment, and joined Physicians from across the Country on December 2, 2015, in a meeting of solidarity to demand its repeal, without funding for medical research, scientific data remains nonexistent.

## Racism by Another Name

A recent CNN Special Report – Race and Reality in America by Catherine E. Shoichet, fully exposes and further supports my claim that xenophobic delusion is real and that WE ARE ALL GUILTY OF PRACTICING IT. Racism is now referred to as racial bias and remains sinful.

In a classic study on race, psychologists staged an experiment with two photographs that produced surprising results.

They showed people a photograph of two White men fighting, one unarmed and another holding a knife. Then they showed another photograph, this one of a White man with a knife fighting an unarmed African-American man. When they asked people to identify the man who was armed in the first picture, most people picked the right one. Yet when they were asked the same question about the second photo, most people -- Black and White -- incorrectly said the Black man had the knife.

Even before it was announced that a grand jury had decided not to indict a White police officer in the shooting death of an unarmed Black teen in Ferguson, Missouri, leaders were calling once again for a national conversation on race.

But, here's why such conversations rarely go anywhere. Scholars and psychologists say Whites and racial minorities speak a different language when they talk about racism.

The knife fight experiment hints at the language gap. Some Whites confine racism to intentional displays of racial hostility. It's the Ku Klux Klan, racial slurs in public, something bad that people do.

But for many racial minorities, that type of racism doesn't matter as much anymore, some scholars say. They talk more about the racism uncovered in the knife fight photos.It doesn't wear a hood, but it causes unsuspecting people to see the world through a racially biased lens... collective delusion.

It's what one Duke University sociologist calls, "racism without racists." Eduardo Bonilla-Silva, who's written a book by that title, says it's a new way of maintaining White domination in places like Ferguson.

"The main problem nowadays is not the folks with the hoods, but the folks dressed in suits," says Bonilla-Silva.

"The more we assume that the problem of racism is limited to the Klan, the birthers, the tea party or to the Republican Party, the less we understand that racial domination is a collective process and we are all in this game."

As people talk about what the grand jury's decision in Ferguson means, Bonilla-Silva and others say,

It's time for Americans to update their language on racism to reflect what it has become and not what it used to be.

"I don't see color."

It's a phrase some White people invoke along with -"I have Black Friends," when a conversation turns to race. Some apply it to Ferguson. They're not particularly troubled by the grand jury's decision to not issue an indictment. The racial identities of Darren Wilson, the White police officer, and Michael Brown, the Black man he killed shouldn't matter, they say. Let the legal system handle the decision without race-baiting. Justice should be colorblind. But is it?

- Science has bad news for anyone who claims to not see race. They're deluding themselves, say several bias experts. A body of scientific research over the past fifty years shows that people notice not only race, but gender, wealth, even weight.

"When babies are as young as three months old, research shows they start preferring to be around people of their own race," says Howard J. Ross, author of *"Everyday Bias,"* which includes the story of the knife fight experiment.

### *Other studies confirm the power of racial bias:*

One study conducted by a Brigham Young University economics professor showed that White NBA referees call more fouls on Black players, and Black referees call more fouls on White players. Another showed that newly released White felons experience better job hunting success than young Black men with no criminal record.

Another famous experiment shows how racial bias can shape a person's economic prospects.

Professors at the University of Chicago and MIT sent 5,000 fictitious resumés in response to 1,300 help wanted ads. Each resumé listed identical qualifications except for one variation; some applicants had Anglo sounding names such as Brendan, while others had Black sounding names such as Jamal. Applicants with Anglo sounding names were 50% more likely to get calls for interviews than their Black sounding counterparts.

- Why should job applicants of color be in doubt about disclosing their racial ethnicity on job applications in fear of not receiving equal opportunity? Employer's proclaimed required reporting excuse is an unjust legal requirement.

- Why do so many employers not value every job applicant with the common decency of a formal notification regarding their application, interview, or rejection status after they've applied for a particular job? Too busy is inexcusable.

Racial biases can in some ways be more destructive than overt racism because they're harder to spot, and therefore harder to combat.

"The idea of calling it racial bias lessens the blow," says Crystal Moten, a history professor at Dickinson College in Carlisle, Pennsylvania.

The first thing we must stop doing is making racism a personal thing and understand that it is a system of advantage based on race.

- Median income among Black Americans is roughly half that of White Americans. But a narrow majority of Whites believe Blacks earn as much money as Whites, and just 37% believe that there's a disparity between the two groups. Likewise, while 56% of Blacks believe Black Americans face significant discrimination, only 16% of Whites agree.

- Many Whites-- including many Millennials -- believe discrimination against Whites is more prevalent than discrimination against Blacks.

But as Nicholas Kristof recently pointed out in The New York Times, the U.S. has a greater wealth gap between Whites and Blacks than South Africa had during apartheid.

- Such racial inequities might seem invisible partly because segregated housing patterns mean that many middle and upper-class Whites live far from poor Blacks.

- "It's also no longer culturally acceptable to be openly racist in the United States," says Bonilla-Silva, author of, "*Racism Without Racists.*"

"Colorblind racism is the new racial music most people dance to," he says. "The new racism is subtle, institutionalized and seemingly nonracial."

### Polls Speaking Truths
In a new **2015**, nationwide poll conducted by CNN and the Kaiser Family Foundation, roughly half of Americans -- **49%** -- say racism is a big problem in society today.

The figure marks a significant shift from four years ago, when over **25%** described racism that way. The percentage is also higher now than it was two decades ago. In 1995, on the heels of the O.J. Simpson trial and just a few years after the Rodney King case surged into the spotlight, 41% of Americans described racism as a big problem.

Is racism on the rise in the United States? Has our awareness changed? Or is it a problem that's been blown out of proportion?

### Go ahead, admit you're a racist.

There's not a one-size-fits-all explanation for the shift. The survey of 1,951 Americans across the country paints a complicated portrait, highlighting some similarities across racial lines, while also exposing gaps that seem to be growing.

But this much is clear.Across the board, in every demographic group surveyed, there are increasing percentages of people who say racism is a big problem. And majorities say racial tensions are on the rise.

In 2008, under much speculation and controversy alleged by his mostly White Republican opponents, the U.S. elected its first Black president in history, Barack Obama. Throughout his first term as president, racial tensions have continuously risen. Since his successful re-election in 2012, National People Polls (across all ethnicities) in 2015 have confirmed that 50% of them believe racism is on the rise which represents a 100% increase from just 25% in 2011.

- America, we have to confront our fears together. Why do 50% of our citizens now believe that racism is worse today than at any other time in the last fifty years?

- Economically, we have been labeled as a deFacto Apartheid Nation by the outside world mainly due to our indisputable wealth inequality gap. But, is there an underlying darkness in the realization that in the next ten years, Eurocentric Americans will become the minority race in America for the first time in its history?

This country of ours is hemorrhaging from the inside out and we are the only ones who can stop it. Not politicians, religious leaders, nor corporate leaders. Most of their agendas are self-centered for personal gain. For the citizens of this country, we must all unite as believers in

Christ, joining heart-to-heart, hand-to-hand geared towards what's best for the common good of all.

- The purpose of life is pursuing a positive value which adds to society. We have to learn to live outside ourselves.

- We are all blessed with many gifts and talents, but only one purpose. Most endeavor to only pursue one talent – "never finding Purpose."

- Peace of mind abounds in the hearts of those who seek the truth. Purpose is therefore simplified and life becomes more fulfilling.

White America's Greatest Delusion: "They Do Not Know It and They Do Not Want to Know It…

It is the innocence which constitutes the crime" *(James Baldwin.)*

"Whoever says he is in the light and hates his brother is still in darkness" (1 John 2:9).

"I have a dream that my four little children will one day live in a nation where they will not be judged by the color of their skin, but by the content of their character" (Dr. Martin Luther King, Jr.).

"When we let freedom ring, when we let it ring from every village and every hamlet, from every state and every city, we will be able to speed up that day when all of God's children, Black men and White men, Jews and Gentiles, Protestants and Catholics, will be able to join hands and sing in the words of the old Negro spiritual, Free at Last! Free at Last! Thank God Almighty, we are Free at Last!" (Dr. Martin Luther King, Jr.)

- *"Freedom is not just a Dream. It's what's on the other side of those fences we build all by ourselves."*

*Xenophobia is considered the root and race is the victim.*

# Chapter 3
# A Patchwork Quilt of Cultures

*The togetherness that binds people is not usually politics or democracy, but more so the sharing of cultures and resources. The U.S. today is a rapidly emerging diverse culture that is becoming more colorized and is transforming from a traditional majority European society to a minority-majority society.*

The U.S. is now starting to resemble a patchwork quilt of different races and cultures and the old guard is alarmed.

**CURRENTLY IN THE U.S. TODAY**, the patchwork is rapidly being rewoven together with various shades and ethnicities of various cultures, however the quilt itself is falling apart at the seams due to xenophobic fears.

The 2016 Republican presidential candidate Jeb Bush while campaigning in Cedar Falls, Iowa, said that multiculturalism is bad for the United States, adding that immigrants who close themselves off from American culture deny themselves access to economic rewards.

Billionaire developer Donald Trump and other 2016 GOP presidential hopefuls have urged newcomers to assimilate. Some have suggested it's their duty.

Recently, in South Carolina, Florida Senator Marco Rubio was interrupted by applause when he said legal status for immigrants should be determined by what they could contribute and whether they want to live in America or whether they want to be American. This is nothing more than forced assimilation.

## CULTURAL UNITY

**Cultural unity is voluntary.** Forced informative assimilation historically has not worked worldwide as proven through various world and national wars. Forceful assimilation at both, the inter and intra levels has caused ethnic conflict and Civil War. It is a practice which qualifies as a crime against humanity. Exclusionism is a prime example of forced assimilation through imposed separation, i.e. apartheid in South Africa and segregation in the U.S. and other parts of the world.

## *Seven Characteristics of Cultural Unity:*

1. Inclusion
2. Respect
3. Tolerance
4. Understanding
5. Compassion
6. Togetherness
7. Reciprocity

Conventional cultural unity is a guarantee for groups who as time goes by, pursue a continually renewed and refreshed higher quality of life, complimented by a variety of cultures with rich traditions. This cultural unity does not attempt to create only one single culture, as this is impractical, but to **maximize the potential of all cultures in order to build the strongest, most reliable national social capital**. It is a two-way system working through the process of sharing values. Knowledge flows through communication channels and all people select for themselves what is timely and important for human development.

Conventional cultural unity emanates from big hearts **accepting** differences and **embracing** differences. It also includes the highest levels of **respect** and **appreciation** people can have for one another. Therefore, the social infrastructure necessary has to be put in place by the government so that more people can develop these types of constructive interactions.

Building Cultural Exchange Institutions is very important. Cultural exchange events allow people to learn from one another. Cultural exchange programs and policies build stronger communities.

Conventional cultural unity does not set out to destroy one culture and build a single culture. Rather, it is a process of allowing all knowledge and cultures to make a contribution, building on that variety to attain a better quality of life. Because each group has something to contribute to the common good, the process of contributing knowledge and culture is a continual process.

Trust between groups starts with a trustworthy diverse political system. Whenever ethnic nature and religion are politicized, it destroys national social capital. Horizontal trust is one of the most vital constituents of a whole healthy country. Horizontal trust means trust between and amongst ethnic groups and their diverse members.

Loss of certainty about the future has often led groups in the past to be suspicious and react negatively towards competing localities, forming attitudes which make the horizontal network and trust weaker due to exclusionism, inequality, injustice, racism, poverty, economic disparity, educational disparity, segregation, unethical politics, inefficient government and overall xenophobic attitudes.

- *"Mankind is like a deck of cards; each card has a distint value and dependence – if one card is missing, the "Deck" is incomplete which prevents us from playing the "Game." Each card's perceived value changes as you begin to play the "Game"- you soon realize that a card's relative value exceeds your initial perception;  same applies with people who unjustly value each other differently until a person demonstrates worth beyond other's perceptions."*

Cultural Unity is considered the *Means* and the *End* is Humanity**.**

God's plan and purpose for Christ was to unite **all things** in Heaven and on Earth (Ephesians 1:9-10).

Therefore, God wants his children united.

The Enemy is Indifference, not Poverty, Racism or Segregation.

# DIVERSITY

The concept of diversity encompasses **inclusion** and **respect**. It means understanding that each individual is unique, and recognizing our individual differences. These can be along the dimensions of race, ethnicity, gender, sexual orientation, socioeconomic status, age, physical abilities, religious beliefs, political beliefs, or other ideologies. It is the exploration of these differences in a safe, positive, and nurturing environment. It is about understanding each other and moving beyond simple tolerance to embracing and celebrating the rich dimensions of diversity contained within each individual.

Diversity is a reality created by individuals and groups from a broad spectrum of demographic and philosophical differences. It is extremely important to support and protect diversity by valuing individuals and groups free from prejudice, and by fostering a climate where equity and mutual respect are intrinsic, while further understanding and recognizing that no one culture is intrinsically superior to another.

Unfortunately, in American society today, diversity is nothing more than a new non-federally regulated twenty-first century Affirmative Action Program of color coding and quota filling at most. This new initiative plays out in almost every form of American life across various public and private enterprises daily from government, schools, businesses, and social organizations alike. Many of these businesses and organizations have even created Diversity Staff Officers to more readily focus on this growing societal challenge. However, while most of their efforts are genuine, there currently exists no Federal nor State laws that mandate minimum compliance criteria which in too many instances just ends up being a corporate marketing program that's socially correct. The same prevailing biased Human Resource policies and personnel restrict effectiveness. Many of these organizations and enterprises still have in place, predominately non-diverse HR departments and ghost policies and procedures that severely handicap true diversity implementation.

In Corporate America today, diversity is the buzz word but not the reality. Corporate America views diversity as a selective representation of race initiative only, which is nothing more than a façade for economic gain with no regard to buying into the sensitivities of inclusion, acceptance, and culture, which are key factors in achieving true diversity anywhere. Representation without inclusion is not representation.

• Corporate America must learn to address – "***The Fear of the Outlander***."

"***Diversity*** does not mean we must have an office that looks like the United Nations cafeteria, but successful growth is dependent upon diverse ideas – diverse ideas normally come from people with "***diverse backgrounds.***" Those with similar backgrounds generally have the same ideas." (*Tom Payne – Future Work*). **Xenophobia** prevents us from embracing and capitalizing on this great opportunity.

We will never achieve true diversity until we resolve the issue of race, sex, and culture. We have simply swept them under the rug while pretending that we are in a post-racial era, while nothing can be further from the truth. ***Race is the number one unresolved issue globally where diversity and inclusion are concerned***. Many people who don't experience this issue, White people, generally disagree even though they continue to practice xenophobic delusion. Less than 10% of the world's population is Eurocentric and 90% are People of Color. This truly means that 90% of the world's population represents various shades of color similar to a patchwork quilt. The dominant growth markets in the world are People of Color in South America, Asia, Africa, the Middle East and India. Even in the U.S., the total school age population will reverse from a Majority – Minority to a Minority – Majority population by 2018. Therefore, in order for Corporate America to remain profitable, they will have to make considerable changes within their existing corporate structures beginning with their HR Departments being demographically transformed to reflect the changing society in which they will become dependent upon for new talent. Secondly, the organizations that truly recognize leveraging the power of a diversity of people within a truly inclusive environment understand that this is the only true source of sustainability, and they will prosper the most.

### *Case in Point:*

Personally, I am most fortunate to have been blessed with the opportunity to bear witness and experience indirectly what "**true diversity**" looks like:

I happen to frequent a certain Library located south of metro Atlanta, Georgia, where a certain group of "Deaf Patrons" meet once per week. This special group is very unique in that they normally meet in an open reading room, where they cluster together and "sign" to one another. What fascinates me is the fact that they are comprised of males and females, 19 – 65 years of age, and various ethnicities to include White, Black, Asian, Hispanic, and Indian – sharing one common bond…being deaf. On several occasions, I have joined them in the reading room and noticed how sensitive, respectful, and compassionate they are toward one another – "everyone is on one accord. " I could'nt help but wonder; why does it take for us to be "handicapped" together i.e. – "stuck-in-the-same-boat together," for us to conquer our xenophobic fears? To me, this experience is the best example of "true diversity" that I have ever seen, read, or heard.

Normal people from all-walks-of-life become engaged in similar opportunities in school, work, and socially, however, their experience becomes a temporary excersise of "tolerance" and as soon as whatever time is up – they all retreat to their isolated silos where life is more comfortable and pleasing…"Xen." Unfortunately, the deaf patrons don't have such a luxury of being able to hide out because most others in our society already have deemed them as being invisible.

- *"We will never overcome our racial problems in America, or the world, until we come to realize that Cultural Unity is not a problem; it's an opportunity to participate in the beauty of diversity."*

## A Thin Line between Diversity and Racial Equality.

The Age of CEO Activism

### *Case in Point:   Starbucks – Champion of Change*
There currently exist in the U.S. today a thin line between diversity and racial equality.

The general consensus in Corporate America today regarding diversity and racial inequality is severely unbalanced. Because race is such an explosive and taboo issue in the U.S., a majority demonstrate support for diversity as a twenty-first century affirmative action supplement, while purposely excluding racial equality from the equation. The sins of slavery are inescapable.

In a recent 2015 publication of Fast Company, Assistant Editor Austin Carr disclosed details of his exclusive interview with Starbucks CEO Howard Schultz regarding their recently launched controversial Race Together Campaign in late March 2015.

Silicon Valley CEO's rose up against restrictive Religious Freedom legislation in Indiana and Arkansas that many believed would discriminate against the gay community (LBGT). Salesforce CEO Mark Benioff led a fleet of high profile tech executives including Apple/PayPal/Walmart in protesting the proposed bills and as a result, State Governors retreated withdrawing the prospective new legislation in fear of job losses. Even though Mr. Schultz and Starbucks equally showed support for LBGT Rights, Mr. Schultz decided not to join his brethren's boycott campaigns. Not because these same powerful corporate leaders had refused just a few weeks earlier to support Mr. Schultz when he launched his company's *Race Together Campaign*, but mainly to protect their efforts from being negatively associated with his campaign and the negative publicity that was still circling it. Mr. Schultz's *Race Together Campaign* was devised to begin to bridge the racial divide by promoting racial equality.

Most outsiders would find it hard to comprehend why Mr. Schultz would even consider jeopardizing his career with such an "EXPLOSIVE RACIAL CAMPAIGN." However, his explanation is revealed as follows: Schultz is aware that people might find it hard to understand where this emotional drive and empathy comes from. He says, "I'm not black, I haven't lived a life in which I was racially profiled, and I wasn't discriminated against because of the color of my skin." He goes on to tells us his outlook was shaped by his upbringing in the Bay View Projects of Brooklyn. He often says he always dreamed of building a company that his late father, who struggled financially throughout life, never had the opportunity to work for.

- Challenging Corporate Culture – "If we just keep going about our business and ringing the Starbucks register every day, then I think we're in a sense part of the problem," Schultz says.

The gist of the program entailed first posting full-page ads in the *New York Times* and the *USA Today*, then asking their baristas nationwide to write race sensitive quotes on the coffee cups of their traditional majority middle upper class customers. The campaign received negative reviews because most of their White customers felt they were personally being targeted as racists. Starbucks did no advertising on social media, mainly because they did not need to, considering they have 22,000 stores that serve a combined 75 million customers per week. Yet, they still generated 2.5 billion negative tweets regarding displeasure with this racial campaign. As a result, the campaign was scaled back and eventually led Mr. Schultz, while speaking at a Racial Inequality Business Forum at Spelman College in April, to state his frustration. "I have not heard from one CEO (Black, White, or Hispanic) offering any help, assistance, or support for our cause."

## *Additional Insights Learned from the Spelman Forum:*
1. Conviction – "I feel we've been called to do this," Schultz says on stage. Along the way, there are going to be some mistakes.

2. Commitment -Schultz boasts that Starbucks was the first U.S. Company to offer comprehensive health-care coverage and stock options to part-time workers.

3. Investment –Their 2015 College Achievement initiative with Arizona State University, which the Company estimates will cost $250 million over the next decade, is another investment in the future.

4. Compassion –Starbucks has a goal of hiring 10,000 military veterans and spouses by 2018.

• Belief – "You can't attract and retain great people if your sole purpose is to make money, because people, especially young people, want a sense of belonging. They want to be part of an organization they really believe is doing great work."You can't create that emotional attachment if you stand for nothing," says Schultz.

• Understanding the magnitude of such a great opportunity Mr. Schultz envisioned due to their broad and diverse customer base, this campaign clearly presented a great opportunity to promote better race relations, elevating racial awareness across national and international cultures with 75 million customers per week worldwide.

• Normally in society, corporate leaders nor otherwise have the courage to stand firm on their convictions in the face of dire opposition. Mr. Schultz therefore must be commended for his efforts to step outside himself in effecting change for the common good, no matter what.

- Kudos to Mr. Howard Schultz, our undisputed corporate champion of change.

Mr. Howard Schultz is surely fitted above and beyond his time.

This is a very high level case study that further supports the fact that gay rights and other diversity rights are resoundingly more politically correct to support by corporate America than highly explosive racial equality rights hands down.

## Case in Point: Sam's Club... The Flip-Side – A Different Perspective – Champion of Change

According to a recent report by Hayley Peterson of Yahoo Finance, Sam's Club CEO Rosalind Brewer sparked controversy on social media after a CNN interview in which she championed diversity and talked about an experience meeting with a supplier who had no representation of women or people of color.

Having stated that she planned to call out a supplier whose team was made up entirely of White men, the Sam's Club CEO is in hot water with White men.

"It has to start with top leadership," Brewer said regarding the way she promotes diversity within her company, Yahoo! Finance reports. "My executive team is very diverse, and I make that a priority. I demand it within my team."

Brewer then added, "Just today we met with a supplier, and the entire other side of the table was all caucasian males. That was interesting. I decided not to talk about it directly with [the supplier's] folks in the room because there were actually no females, like, levels down. So I'm going to place a call to him."

The comment caused uproar on Twitter, with several people calling Brewer's comments racist toward White men. Yahoo! Finance points out that Brewer's executive team is made up of eight people, four of whom are White men. But that didn't stop the Twitter mob, which proclaimed it had spent its last dollar at the big-box wholesale store.

Several took to the store's Facebook page to voice their outrage:

- "As a White male I'm deeply offended by the remarks of your employee," one person wrote on Sam's Club's Facebook page. "We will not be patronizing Sam's Club until this is corrected."

- "Racism is alive and well in America," another user wrote. "I will never spend a dime in a Sam's club!"

- Those offended by Brewer's comments are going to have a tough time shopping, since Wal-Mart, Sam's Club's parent company is standing behind Brewer's statement.

"For years, we've asked our suppliers to prioritize the talent and diversity of their sales teams calling on our company," Wal-Mart CEO Doug McMillon told Yahoo! Finance.

"Roz was simply trying to reiterate that we believe diverse and inclusive teams make for a stronger business," he said. "That's all there is to it, and I support that important ideal."

- This is exactly the type of top leadership that is required as Ms. Brewer not only described above, but also acted upon, with full support throughout their corporate family. This is exactly the same type of uncompromised efforts we continuously advocate as missing in Corporate America today.

  Kudos to the Walmart leadership team…our big retail champion of change.

This is yet another resounding example of how on the premise, Ms. Brewer responded to the lack of visible diversity, however, in the face of mainstream America it became viewed as promoting racial equality.

## *Case in Point: Georgia Prosper Coalition - A different approach – Economic Solidarity.*

The Georgia Senate overwhelmingly passed the Georgia Religious Freedom Restoration Act on March 5, 2015, that opponents say will give businesses and individuals a license to discriminate against LGBT people and anyone else under the guise of religious freedom. This Bill is very similar to the Bill's that were passed in Arkansas and Indiana that generated the firestorm of CEO activism started by Salesforce CEO Mark Beinoff, which setoff major corporate boycotts that forced both respective Governors to modify the Bill's in fear of job losses.

Georgia's Bill was tabled by a House Judiciary Committee, but it could be revived as soon as the State Legislature convenes on January 11, 2016. As a result, in a show of solidarity, on January 6, 2015, many of Georgia's largest 100 employers in anticipation of a battle with State legislature, formed and launched the Georgia Prospers Coalition as a safeguard of separation from the restrictive anti-gay implications that pose the threat of causing a potential $1.5 billion loss of revenue for all Georgia businesses. These are the same corporations that uniformly continue existing practices of racial exclusion in leadership and hiring initiatives that promote true diversity in regards to race,which in and of itself poses a far greater economic risk.

Again, yet another high level case study that even though it takes a different approach in forming a Corporate Coalition to move jobs further supports the fact that gay rights and other diversity rights are unequivocally resoundingly more politically correct to support by Corporate America than highly explosive racial equality rights.

- Is it possible that gay rights are far easier for many corporate leaders to support because many profess to be LBGT themselves?

- Is it also possible that racial equality is deemed too explosive to promote because there currently exists gross disparities in minority leadership representation amongst the corporate elite?

  *"Diversity is politically correct and morally pleasing."*
  *"Racial equality is politically explosive and morally taboo."*

History has taught us that laws, policies, and procedures are deemed ineffective in influencing compassionate **change of heart** in the minds of the power structure. The heart generates feelings that the mind converts to thoughts.

# Chapter 4

# Collective Delusion

*Every Society has Systems that, over centuries, have been meticulously modified and manipulated to benefit the "Power Structure." The general public has continually accepted these changes due to natural innate abilities as humans to adapt to almost any living condition. The same trait that enables us to survive also suppresses us, and enslaves us. Eventually, as the "Power" Structure continues to pass down these restrictive policies, the masses tend to conform, adjust, and accept them without challenge as the new norm.*

## Structural Collective Delusion

A RECENT QUOTE FROM THE Four Horsemen Documentary 2012, confirms that in most Societies, The Elite stay in power not by controlling the means of production (money), but by controlling our cognitive map, the way we think. It's not so much about what is said in public, but what's left undebated and unsaid.

## Case in Point: *As quoted from The Four Horsemen Documentary*

- "One of the greatest Frameworks of Western Civilization that shapes the way we think today is the Hollywood Movie construction which affects the way people view themselves and tell stories:

| Cultural Pattern: | **Beginning** | **Middle** | **End** |
|---|---|---|---|
| Hollywood Movie: | Drama | Tension | Resolution |
| Financial Crisis: | LehmanBrothers | BernieMadoff | Bailouts |

Even though 80% of the American public was against the **Financial Bailouts**, the Government declared that big banks and Corporations were "*Too Big to Fail*" and proceeded to bail them out to the tune of $1.4 trillion (Bush Administration - $700 billion; Obama Administration

- $700 billion). The overall Financial Crisis left the masses in shock, feeling helpless and delusional as to the root cause. This is a financial systemic problem that renders all beneficiaries guilty. To date, not one Wall Street Executive or Big Bank Executive has been prosecuted for their destructive financial misdeeds."

## Case in Point:

Richard Adams of *The Guardian* captured the following quote by Lloyd Blankfein, CEO of Goldman Sachs (GS), providing the following justifications for their firm's obvious unethical practices when questioned by the U.S. Senate on April 27, 2009:

According to pre-released testimony, the head of Goldman Sachs, Lloyd Blankfein, admitted that his bank failed to raise the alarm about excesses in the mortgage industry and got involved in overly complex derivatives deals that fueled perceptions of Wall Street running out of control. Blankfein will tell the committee that the Securities and Exchange Commission's $1bn (£647m) fraud case against his firm marks a low point in his career (Subject lawsuit was eventually settled in the Government's favor for $1.2 billion in August 2014); and an additional $3.8 billion in January 2016 - $5 billion total settlement. In its mind the Bank has done nothing wrong, nothing whatsoever. In fact, it believes quite the reverse: that its actions are beyond reproach, barring a few choice emails that they'd rather hadn't been made public, and that GS is merely an honest market-maker.

The thing is, the Senators don't understand how a modern Investment Bank works – or rather, now that they've found out, they are shocked. That a reputable bank can play both sides of the market, like the mob telling one of its boxers to take a fall, selling investments at the same time as selling those clients and investments short, is what has shocked them. To the Senators though, that's betting against their own clients. According to Goldman, that's "reducing risk."

## Government/Wall Street Bedfellows:

According to a *New York Times* article by Gretchen Morgenson and Don Van Natta, Jr. on August 8, 2009, the following more disturbing Financial Crisis logistical relationships are disclosed:

"Before he became President George W. Bush's Treasury Secretary in 2006, Henry M. Paulson, Jr. agreed to hold himself to a higher ethical standard than his predecessors. He not only sold all his holdings in Goldman Sachs, the Investment Bank he ran, but also specifically said that he would avoid any substantive interaction with Goldman executives for his entire term unless he first obtained an ethics waiver from the government.

Mr. Paulson did not say when he received a waiver, but copies of two waivers he received from the White House counsel's office and the Treasury Department show they were issued on the afternoon of September 17, 2008. That date was in the middle of the most perilous week of the financial crisis and a day after the government agreed to lend $85 billion to the American International Group (A.I.G.), which used the money to pay off Goldman and other big banks that were financially threatened by A.I.G.'s potential collapse.

It is common, of course, for regulators to be in contact with market participants to gather valuable industry intelligence, and financial regulators had to scramble very quickly last fall to address an unprecedented crisis. In those circumstances, it would have been difficult for anyone to follow routine guidelines.

During the week of the A.I.G. bailout alone, the calendars show Mr. Paulson and Mr. Blankfein spoke two dozen times, far more frequently than Mr. Paulson did with any other Wall Street executives. On September 17, the day Mr. Paulson secured his waivers, he and Mr. Blankfein spoke five times. Two of the calls occurred before Mr. Paulson's waivers were granted."

## *Inevitable Questions*
Concerns about potential conflicts of interest were perhaps inevitable during this financial crisis, which has been deemed the worst since the Great Depression. In the weeks before Mr. Paulson obtained the waivers, "Treasury lawyers raised questions about whether he had conflicts of interest," a senior government official said.

# Political Collective Delusion

Indeed, Mr. Paulson helped decide the fates of a variety of financial companies, including two longtime Goldman rivals, Bear Stearns and Lehman Brothers, before his ethics waivers were granted. Ad hoc actions taken by Mr. Paulson and officials at the Federal Reserve, like letting Lehman fail andcompensating A.I.G.'s trading partners, continue to confound some market participants and members of Congress.

"I think it's clear he had a conflict of interest," Mr. Stearns, the congressman, said in an interview. "He was covering himself with this waiver because he knew he had a conflict of interest with his telephone calls and with his actions. Even though he had no money in Goldman, he had a vested interest in Goldman's success, in terms of his own reputation and historical perspective."

Critics say, adding to questions about Mr. Paulson's roleis the fact that Goldman Sachs was among a group of banks that received substantial government assistance during the turmoil. Goldman not only received $13 billion in taxpayer money as a result of the A.I.G. bailout, but also was given permission at the height of the crisis to convert from an investment firm to a national bank, giving it easier access to federal financing in the event it came under greater financial pressure.

Goldman also won federal debt guarantees and received $10 billion under the Troubled Asset Relief Program. It benefited further when the Securities and Exchange Commission suddenly changed its rules governing stock trading, barring investors from being able to bet against Goldman's shares by selling them short.

Now that the company's crisis has passed, Goldman has rebounded more markedly than its rivals. It has paid back the $10 billion in government assistance, with interest, and exited the federal debt guarantee program. It recently reported second-quarter profits of $3.44 billion, putting its employees on track to earn record bonuses this year of approximately $700,000 each, on average.

## *Goldman's Windfall*
Mr. Paulson has disavowed any involvement in the decision to use taxpayer funds to make Goldman and A.I.G.'s trading partners'whole.

However, according to two senior government officials involved in the discussions about an A.I.G. bailout and several other people who attended those meetings speaking anonymously because of confidentiality agreements, the government's decision to rescue A.I.G was made collectively by Mr. Paulson, officials from the Federal Reserve and other financial regulators in meetings at the New York Federal Reserve over the weekend of September 13-14, 2008.

Over that weekend, according to a former senior government official involved in the discussions, Mr. Paulson said that he had been warned by lawyers for the Treasury Department not to contact Goldman executives directly. The former official said Mr. Paulson told him he had disregarded the advice because the "crisis" required action.

On September 16, 2008, the day the government agreed to inject billions into A.I.G., Mr. Paulson personally called Robert B. Willumstad, A.I.G.'s chief executive, and dismissed him. Mr. Paulson's involvement in the decision to rescue A.I.G. is also supported by an e-mail message sent by Scott G. Alvarez, general counsel at the Federal Reserve Board to Robert Hoyt, a Treasury legal counsel, that same day.

Since that time, the government's commitment to A.I.G. has swelled to $173 billion. A recent report from the Government Accountability Office questioned whether taxpayers would ever be repaid the money loaned to what was once the world's largest insurance company. AIG did repay all of the borrowed tax payer money back plus interest in 2013, but have since filed a lawsuit against the Federal Reserve because they did not like the terms and interest rate of their Bailout Agreement. This is social arrogance personified. What would they have done without the Bailout? They would have filed bankruptcy like their former trading partner, Lehman Brothers...

## Constant Contact

In the ethics agreement that Mr. Paulson signed in 2006, he wrote, "I believe that these steps will ensure that I avoid even the appearance of a conflict of interest in the performance of my duties as Secretary of the Treasury."

While that agreement barred him from dealing on specific matters involving Goldman, he spoke with Mr. Blankfein at other pivotal moments in the crisis before receiving waivers. Mr. Paulson's schedule from 2007 and 2008 show that he spoke with Mr. Blankfein, who was his successor as Goldman's chief, twenty-six times before receiving a waiver. At the height of the financial crisis, Mr. Paulson spoke far more often with Mr. Blankfein than any other executive, according to entries in his calendar. Moreover, because his schedule included only phone calls made through Mr. Paulson's office at the Treasury, they provide only a partial picture of his communications. They do not reflect calls he made on his cellphone or from his home telephone.

According to the schedule, Mr. Paulson's contact with Mr. Blankfein began even before the height of the crisis last fall. During August 2007, for example, when the market for asset-backed commercial paper was seizing up, Mr. Paulson spoke with Mr. Blankfein thirteen times. Mr. Paulson placed twelve of those calls.

## Corporate Socialist Politics

According to a recent article published in the *Huffington Post* by Zach Carter, Senior Political Economy Reporter, in WASHINGTON, DC, House Republicans on Monday unveiled legislation that would decriminalize a broad swath of corporate malfeasance, a move that injects white-collar crime issues into the thus far bipartisan agenda on criminal justice reform.

The public debate over criminal justice reform has focused on reducing severe sentences for nonviolent drug offenses. But some influential conservative voices, including the billionaire Koch Brothers and the Heritage Foundation, have quietly advocated for curbing prosecution of Corporate offenses as well.

The House bill would eliminate a host of white-collar crimes where the damaging acts are *merely* reckless, negligent or grossly negligent. If enacted, it would make it more difficult for federal authorities to pursue executive wrongdoing, from financial fraud to environmental pollution.

Large, complex corporations can diffuse responsibility for illegal activity, which can make it difficult for prosecutors to prove that executives knowingly and willfully violated the law. CEOs can also pressure lower-level employees to violate the law without explicitly telling them to do so by demanding profits or other results that are impossible to reach without breaking the law. Under the current law, however, corporate crime prosecutions are already relatively rare and frequently skip over executives and other top managers. When employees are charged, it's often lower-level employees.

The Justice Department has been heavily criticized for its weak enforcement against corporate crimes during the Obama years. No Wall Street executives were charged for the misconduct that caused the 2008 financial crisis.

Under the House bill, high-level corporate wrongdoers would have even less to worry about.

## Adding Insult to Injury:

According to various confirmed sources, Five of the largest U.S. Banks (assets $50 billion +), including Bank of America, J.P. Morgan Chase, and Wells Fargo who received billions of U.S. taxpayer bail-out money under the Too-Big-To-Fail scandal, remain non-compliant with provisions under the 2010 Dodd Frank Wall Strreet Reform Law. Under the Law, banks with excess of $50 billion in assets are required to maintain higher cash holdings in addition to developing "Living Will (bankruptcy plans)" in the event of failure; the Federal Reserve Board and FDIC after recent audits, have deemed the respective Bank's plans as being "Non-credible/ Non Compliant and have thus granted them all an extension through October 1, 2016 to comply.

## Cultural Collective Delusion

I have personally interviewed hundreds of U.S. citizens over the last several years from all walks-of-life and across all cultures and most seem to agree resoundingly with the fact that racism and other xenophobic practices are alive and well and not only practiced against outside cultures but inter-culturally as well based on skin color, social class, religion, sexual orientation, and political affiliation. However, *they all firmly deny that they participate in such practices. This is cultural collective delusion.* They further concur that the current US socio-economic systems heavily promote, control, and support all of the negative outcomes trending today in society of which the citizens themselves TAKE NO RESPONSIBILITY.

As a general rule, the U.S. and most other Societies operate on a Structural-Functional Theory also known as the Consensus Theory of Order which is devised to benefit the *most powerful group* of a particular society. The main foundation of this System is that there must exist a Social Structure (Primary Structure) and Values and Ideas (Secondary Structure) whereby the Values and Ideas are used to Justify and Preserve the existing Social Structure,therefore the less privileged in the Society will accept the unequal distribution of the good things of life, including power, status, and wealth.

Values and Ideas are simply an extension of the power struggle between Social Groups which goes on continuously. Everyday there are battles to determine whose values and ideas will dominate the various Institutions of Society. USUALLY THE VALUES OF THE MOST POWERFUL GROUP PREVAIL. This is also known as the Conflict Theory which stresses who gets what - Who gets Richer and Who gets Screwed. In most societies worldwide, one dominant group prevails over the others. In the U.S., Minority Groups are significantly underrepresented in the "Halls of Power."

The Consensus and Conflict Theories are unified and complement one another to create a Structured System of Order that tolerates compromise, but only when it benefits the dominant Power Group the most. Historical structural racism is real.

# Chapter 5

# Character Always Comes to Light Under Trial

*As defined, character is the mental and moral qualities distinctive to an individual, but in application…it translates into - What you do when you don't think anyone is watching.*

**"PEOPLE WILL EVEN ABANDON** *their Religion if it conflicts with their economic interests"*

-Samuel Eliot Morison

1. During Slavery, Evangelical Religion increased because slave owners felt guilty trying to justify slavery while remaining Christians and following the Bible.

2. During Prohibition (1920 – 1933), millions of Americans denounced their religious beliefs entirely in order to continue to consume alcohol illegally. More alcohol was consumed during Prohibition than at any time prior to.

3. In 1962, with the abolishment of prayer and religious expression in Public Schools and other Public places, the U.S. demonstrated a resounding withdrawal from her Founding Religious Principles also known as "Separation of Religion and State."

4. In 1973, with the Legalizing of Abortions, the U.S. continued to stray further away from Religious Belief. This has resulted in excess of 53 million Abortions in the U.S. since 1973.

5. In July 2015, the U.S. Supreme Court legalized Gay Marriage in all fifty States, confirming our new religious status of being a Secular Nation.

## *Case in Point: Following Godly Conviction*

MOREHEAD, Ky. — Defying the Supreme Court and saying she was acting under God's authority, a county clerk in Kentucky denied marriage licenses to gay couples on Tuesday, September 1, 2015, stating that she is obligated to follow God's laws versus Man's.

As a result of being in direct contempt of a court order, she was persecuted and finally jailed on Thursday, September 3, 2015, thus becoming the first U.S. Citizen to be jailed for their religious beliefs. She was eventually released six days later. Upon returning to work, she was officially allowed to remove her signature from previously issued marriage licenses and would not be required to sign any future licenses which has no effect on the validity of the licenses as agreed upon by the Supreme Court.

## Age of Religious Leader Activism

The first Christian leaders did not take sides on political issues. Jesus and his disciples took a neutral stand on political issues, refraining from engaging in political discussions with kings and other dignitaries by simply reminding them that their Kingdom was not part of this world (John 18:36).

Today, religion seems to influence nearly every aspect of secular life. Religious Leaders, instead of reflecting more critically on devising ways to become more effective Spiritual Leaders, are becoming more vocally involved in all sorts of political, business, and economic issues that tend to further divide people rather than unite them.

In 2013, Jorge Mario Bergoglio became the first Jesuit Pope, as Francis. He challenged trickle-down economics and questioned the absolute autonomy of markets, revealing that some people continue to defend trickle-down theories which assume that economic growth, encouraged by a free market, will inevitably succeed in bringing about greater justice and inclusiveness in the world. Pope Francis wrote in the papal statement, "This opinion, which has never been confirmed by facts, expresses a crude and naive trust in the goodness of those wielding economic power and in the sacralized workings of the prevailing economic system. "Meanwhile," he added, "the excluded are still waiting."

Trickle-down Economics also known as the Horse and Sparrow Theory is born out of Neoclassical Economics Theories of the late eighteenth and nineteenth centuries which has been the dominant paradigm of economic reasoning in English-speaking countries since the 1950s. In this unjust System of Economic Structure, a sort of Plutocracy exists in that the Country is governed by the Rich which becomes Socialism for the rich and becomes Capitalism for the poor as a form of enslavement. This is a "Goliath" of the world.

Pope Francis directly addressed and challenged the U.S. Congress on September 24, 2015. "Each son or daughter of a given country has a mission, a personal and social responsibility. Your own responsibility as members of Congress is to enable this country, by your legislative activity, to grow as a nation. You are the face of its people, their representatives. You are called to defend and preserve the dignity of your fellow citizens in the tireless and demanding pursuit of the common good, for this is the chief aim of all politics. A political society endures when it seeks, as a vocation, to satisfy common needs by stimulating the growth of all its members, especially those in situations of greater vulnerability or risk. Legislative activity is always based on care for the people. To this you have been invited, called and convened by those who elected you.

• This year marks the one hundred and fiftieth anniversary of the assassination of President Abraham Lincoln, the guardian of liberty, who labored tirelessly that this nation, under God, [might] have a new birth of freedom. Building a future of freedom requires love of the common good and cooperation in a spirit of subsidiarity and solidarity.

The challenges facing us today call for a renewal of that spirit of cooperation, which has accomplished so much good throughout the history of the United States. The complexity, the gravity and the urgency of these challenges demand that we pool our resources and talents, and resolve to support one another, with respect for our differences and our convictions of conscience. Such cooperation is a powerful resource in the battle to eliminate new global forms of slavery, born of grave injustices which can be overcome only through new policies and new forms of social consensus.

*If politics must truly be at the service of the human person, it follows that it cannot be a slave to the economy and finance."*

Unfortunately, this is exactly one of America's biggest socioeconomic challenges today

Ironically, several potential contenders for the presidency in 2016 are economic conservatives who are also Catholic. In the past, Liberal Catholic Groups have taken aim at what they view as the overly stingy policies of such Republican Conservatives, who have little regard for the role of government in redistributing income. Though, overwhelmingly conflicting views between Conservatives and Catholics exist, these same Conservatives profess to be devout Catholics. This is collective delusion.

## *Socialist Arrogance*

Donald Trump, the front-running American Republican presidential candidate, has publicly attacked all minorities - more specifically: Blacks, Latinos, and Muslims which has generated repeated protest since June 2015.

The following excerpt is from June 16, 2015, while Mr. Trump was on his campaign trail in Manhattan, New York,

"Sadly, the American dream is dead, but if I get elected president I will bring it back," he said, "Bigger, better and stronger than ever before."

Most of his wrath was directed at Mexico, which he accused of bringing their worst people to America, including criminals and rapists.

Trump promised that as president, one of his first actions would be to build a great, great wall on our southern border and that he would make Mexico pay for the wall.

There were no mass demonstrations in the streets, but Latino protesters amassed online. Their focus? The hurtful anti-Mexican comments made by Republican presidential candidate Donald Trump.

Latinos gathered in social media circles to condemn, plot and retaliate against Trump with such fervor, they caused three multi-billion dollar media companies to back away from him: Univision, NBC and Televisa.

Macy's retail stores also announced it was removing Trump merchandising from its stores after 700,000 people signed a Move On.org petition.

## Hispanic Religious Leaders Inactivism

National Latino Evangelical Coalition founder Gabriel Salguero, called Trump's comments xenophobic. Calling Trump xenophobic isn't a stretch, but demanding action requires courage. If one expects consequences to be meted out by any organization, by any class of people in the Latino community, one would expect its religious leaders to speak up about consequences.

The other Latino evangelical political group, the National Hispanic Christian Leadership Conference (NHCLC) led by Samuel Rodriguez, said absolutely nothing. This organization has trumpeted and oversold its political abilities for over a decade with claims made by self-appointed leaders like Rev. Sam Rodriguez that they would deliver millions of votes to candidates that supported their agenda. The stark reality is that Latinos have not delivered in proportion to their billion-dollar buying power.

- Contrary to Popular Belief (delusion), inaction by both of these highly regarded Hispanic religious leaders, actually represents the exact same position Jesus and His disciples took regarding political issues.

## *Trump Supports Physical Racial Attacks*

After viewing a video of his supporters beating up a Black Lives Matter protester on November 21, 2015, in Birmingham, Alabama, Donald Trump suggested they may have done the right thing. The protester, a Black Man, reportedly started chanting Black Lives Matter at a Trump rally and rally attendees swarm around the man, kicking and punching him as he curls up on the ground.

Reports of Trump supporters launching violent and racist attacks have become fairly commonplace. Another recent rally took a dark turn when attendees shoved and spat on immigration advocates. The following week, Trump supporters were filmed dragging and kicking an immigration activist while others yelled U-S-A! U-S-A!

After a slew of these highly publicized incidents, Trump's campaign began corralling the media and refused to allow reporters into the crowd at rallies.

## Black Religious Leader Activism

On November 30, 2015, dozens of African American Pastors gathered behind closed doors with GOP frontrunner Donald Trump at his office in New York City. The Trump campaign originally told the press the pastors were going to endorse him, despite the fact they had never promised to do so. Organizers chalked this up to miscommunication.

Kenyatta Gilbert, an associate professor at Howard University's Divinity School, characterized the pastors attending the closed-door meeting, many of whom are gospel artists, Black mega-church personalities, and televangelists, as prosperity preachers who teach that faith and positive thinking will lead to material wealth.

One must ask the question, is there any other legitimate reason why these religious leaders would agree to meet with this presidential frontrunner even though they clearly disagree with his agenda and tactics?

### *Muslim Ban*

According to a CNN report on December 8, 2015, a San Bernardino Muslim terrorist attack left fourteen dead. Republican presidential front runner Donald Trump called for barring all Muslims from entering the United States. "Donald J. Trump is calling for a total and complete shutdown of Muslims entering the United States until our country's representatives can figure out what is going on," a campaign press release said. Trump, who has previously called for surveillance of mosques, said he was open to establishing a database for all Muslims living in the US. His controversial message comes in the wake of a deadly mass shooting in San Bernardino, California, by suspected ISIS sympathizers the day after President Barack Obama asked the country not to turn against one another in fear.

Donald Trump's Muslim ban rallies religious leaders against him.

## *A fast response from across faiths*

A December 8, 2015, *New York Times* article by Elizabeth Dias, captured the moment as follows,

"On the second night of Hanukkah, the eve of Pope Francis' Holy Year of Mercy, and the same night that the Catholic archbishop of Indianapolis rejected his governor's request to stop resettling a Syrian refugee family, Donald Trump had a religious message of his own: a call for a complete and total ban on Muslims entering the U.S.

Unsurprisingly, Trump stood largely alone. Backlash from religious leaders of all stripes was immediate.

- Nihad Awad, executive director of the Council on American-Islamic Relations, compared Trump to the leader of a lynch mob. Serene Jones, president of Union Theological Seminary in New York City, tweeted this message to @realDonaldTrump: Jesus and the Constitution agree. No hate-based, religious discrimination! No discrimination, period.

- The National Latino Evangelical Coalition pushed the hashtag #StopTrumpXenophobia

- Anthony Evans, president of the National Black Church Initiative, called for Trump to step out of the race. Saying in a statement, "We will oppose him and others through our moral goodness."

- Russell Moore, president of the Southern Baptist Convention's Ethics and Religious Liberty Coalition, Moore wrote on his blog shortly after Trump's announcement. "A government that can close the borders to all Muslims simply on the basis of their religious belief can do the same thing for evangelical Christians. We must have security and we must have order. But we must not trade soul freedom for an illusion of winning."

- Jonathan Greenblatt, who leads the Anti-Defamation League, agreed. "The U.S. was founded as a place of refuge for those fleeing religious persecution, and religious pluralism is core to our national identity. A plan that singles out Muslims and denies them entry to the U.S. based on their religion is deeply offensive and runs contrary to our nation's deepest values."

Obama Administration condemns Trump's proposal

Obama's deputy national security adviser Ben Rhodes reacted to Trump's call Monday on CNN, calling it totally contrary to our values as Americans and pointed to the Bill of Rights' protection of freedom of religion. He also pointed to the extraordinary contributions Muslim Americans have made to the U.S.

# Chapter 6
# The Evolution of Capitalism

*Capitalism as defined is a system of economics based on private ownership of the means of production, and the production of goods and services for profit based on supply and demand which on the surface looks fairly reasonable and practical, but in reality through modern day market manipulation and consumer exploitation, it has created a* **"Shallow Hall Effect** *– A mental state of materialistic existence that is fueled by an unconscious desire to belong i.e. herd mentality, whereby the masses are duped into believing that buying more of what you don't need will bring you acceptance, authentication, and happiness...keeping-up-with-the-Jones."*

**EDWARD LOUIS JAMES BARNAYS** (November 22, 1891 – March 9, 1995), was an Austrian-American pioneer in the field of public relations and propaganda. He was referred to in his obituary as the father of public relations. He combined the ideas of Gustave Le Bon and Wilfred Trotter on crowd psychology with the psychoanalytical ideas of his uncle, Sigmund Freud.

"Barnays" felt this manipulation was necessary in society, which he regarded as irrational and dangerous as a result of the herd instinct. The conscious and intelligent manipulation of the organized habits and opinions of the masses is an important element in democratic society. Those who manipulate this unseen mechanism of society constitute an invisible government which is the true ruling power of our country. We are governed, our minds are molded, our tastes formed, our ideas suggested, largely by men we have never heard of.

This is a logical result of the way in which our democratic society is organized. Vast numbers of human beings must cooperate in this manner if they are to live together as a smoothly functioning society. In almost every act of our daily lives, whether in the sphere of politics or business, in our social conduct or our ethical thinking, we are dominated by the relatively small number of persons who understand the mental processes and social patterns of the masses. It is they who pull the wires which control the public mind.

Modern consumer capitalism has artfully mastered the techniques of the manipulation of the psyche and has even turned the practice into an industry in and of itself: advertising, public relations and marketing. Advanced capitalism's ability to exploit general tendencies in the human mind, particularly the subconscious mind has led to a proliferation of a sophisticated propaganda racket that shapes public opinion and governs people's behavior.

Edward Bernays saw this development in a highly positive light. He argued that intelligent manipulation of the organized habits and opinions of the masses is an important element in democratic society, and that somewhat paradoxically to any vision of 'democratic' society, the 'socially necessary' manipulators constitute an invisible government which is the true ruling power in our country. Not the President. Not Congress. Not the Supreme Court.

## *The Birth of Consumerism also known as Capitalism*

Appropriately and true to his word, Bernays managed to rebrand his position as a propagandist by euphemistically renaming propaganda, public relations. The advertising and marketing industries have developed tried and tested techniques of selling commodities. The methods stem from the psychoanalytical idea of tapping into the subconscious, appealing to repressed desires, sublimating them through buying power and promises of personal fulfillment, empowerment, pleasure, and strength through expenditure.

We find our identities in what we buy and express ourselves through the commodities we own. Buying has become a process of self-affirmation and what we buy determines not only our status, but can signify our belonging to a group, our belief in an ideal or our loyalty to a brand. Consumer trends, fashion and fads are a testament to the relevance of "**the herd instinct**" that Freud examines in group psychology and the analysis of the ego. In an appraisal of the work of Gustave Le Bon, Freud states, "we have an impression of a state in which an individual's separate emotion and personal intellectual act are too weak to anything by themselves and are absolutely obliged to wait till they are reinforced through being repeated in a similar way in the other members of the group."

- **Rampant consumerism**, from a psychoanalytical point of view, can be seen as an expression of libidinal desires sublimated with 'retail therapy' or the instinctual drive of human beings to be part of 'the herd'. The success of advertising is measured by its ability to convince potential consumers that an ownership of a certain product will guarantee them a place in that herd or that their fears, anxieties, and internal conflicts can be resolved and pleasure attained through the simple act of buying.

- **Capitalism entered a qualitatively new globalizing phase in the 1950s**. As the **electronic revolution** got underway, significant changes began to occur in the productivity of capitalist factories, systems of extraction and processing of raw materials, product design, marketing and distribution of goods and services. **Second**, the technical and social relations that structured the **mass media** all over the world made it very easy for new consumerist lifestyles to become the dominant motif for these media sources, which became in time extraordinarily efficient vehicles for the broadcasting of the cultural ideology of consumerism globally.

*The growth capitalistic society demands that we make consumption a way of life.*

## Age of Decadence

The Baby Boomer generation was born into this Age of Decadence (don't give a damn) also known as the1950's and have thus broken the Unspoken *Intergenerational Contract* through uncontrolled acts of unfettered consumerism, spiraling house prices, pursuit of youth, acquiring vast amounts of unnecessary luxuries, and *squandering future generations' inheritance* by leaving them with an unserviceable lifetime of debts. All for the sake of keeping up with the Joneses, which is nothing more than the things you own that end up owning you.

- "No generation has the right to contract debts greater than can be paid off during the course of itsownexistence."(President Lincoln).

Many of the world's richest countries are experiencing historic levels of income inequality. Even in the developing world, there are emerging concerns about whether workers will benefit from their countries' increasing prosperity. Economic inequality is the number one prevailing attribute of a plutocratic society, a society which is governed by the socialist rich who promote self-serving neoclassical economic policies of capitalism.

The world economy has been built either on military commercialization or on producing items that most people don't need. But, we've become delusional about separating needs and wants due to our need for social acceptance.

## Socialism and Capitalism Are Inseparable

### *Case in Point:*

According to a very insightful article published in *Nation of Change* by Michael Payne: "*Where American Socialism and Capitalism Blend Together Perfectly*"

"First, we have the capitalist sector of America, the massive defense industry corporations who make the weapons of war that enrich their bottom lines. Then, we have the U.S. military which takes this weaponry and uses it in the pursuit of its agenda of endless war. Together, they form that large and successful consortium that is continuously funded by American taxpayers and administered by the U.S. Government" (Payne 2015).

Yes, we constantly hear many Americans condemning socialism and how terrible a system it is and yet the gigantic U.S. military organization that stretches across this entire planet is a living example of socialism in America. And there is no question that the vast majority of the American people are solidly behind it.

A typical definition of socialism is an economic concept that advocates public/government ownership and management of all resources. Well, that's it. That's exactly what the U.S. military is and here is why:

Those who serve in the military have government-guaranteed jobs as long as they don't violate certain rules and regulations. There are no unemployment rolls. Those who follow reasonable rules and stay out of trouble will not lose their jobs; and their jobs cannot be outsourced.

The U.S. military is fully funded by American taxpayers and administered by the Government. Its members and families are provided with free base housing and those living off base are given allowances to help cover their housing costs. They receive free health care, including eye care and dental benefits. Most members are provided with an education by attending various military schools where they receive sophisticated electronic training and acquire other high-level skills they can use when and if they decide to go back to civilian life. All members can receive a pension if they remain in the military for the time required. Members can take part in the Food Stamp program and they can use the money in base commissaries where prices are considerably lower than those in civilian stores. Those who qualify can receive up to $500 per month under the FSSA, the Family Subsistence Supplemental Allowance Program. In recent years, military members have received over $100 million annually from that program and that cost continues to increase.

Now let's shift our attention to the capitalism element of this close, tight-knit relationship. Actually, this specific sector of American Capitalism, the defense industry, has a socialist element built into it because these corporations depend greatly upon a steady stream of military contracts from the government. We might accurately describe it as a quasi-capitalist/socialist industry. These corporations are, in effect, receiving a form of government welfare. In fact, if it were not for the government, most of them would not exist.

While Capitalism and Socialism, in theory, are like the difference between night and day, this Military/ Corporate alliance dispels that concept in that these two entities totally complement each other. They pursue intertwined objectives and work in unison to maintain the vast U.S. military empire.

Here are some concrete examples of how this capitalistic/socialist consortium operates and how it has advanced its agenda of endless war at the expense of the America taxpayer.

We hear politicians constantly talking about waste in government, but they can't seem to grasp the fact that the biggest area of ongoing waste is found in military spending. So let's talk about our national debt and how military spending contributes so greatly to its constant growth. The U.S. National debt was $5.7 trillion in 2000. After the Bush War on Iraq and the Afghan War, which together cost over $3 trillion, along with other wasteful military spending, this debt has now reached $18.9 trillion. An increase of $13.2 trillion, or if you can believe it, 332% in less than two decades.

The U.S. spends far more on defense and security than any other nation and since September 11, 2001, the Department of Defense (DOD) budget has increased steadily. As of 2014, the DOD budget reached an all-time high of $763 Billion which represented 20% of the total federal budget. One has to ask himself, why does the U.S. spend considerably more on defense and security than any other nation?

- Is it because all of her strong arm international democracy advances are now starting to come to light with the tremendous increase of terroristic activity imposed against the U.S.?

- Is the U.S. paranoid in guilt over its dark past of imposing inhumane transgressions against disenfranchised nations?

These are also examples of how it has wasted hundreds of billions and trillions of taxpayer dollars, a great portion of which is badly needed for America's domestic needs:

The massive U.S. Embassy built in Baghdad cost $750 million. Why in creation did those in Washington think they needed to construct the world's largest embassy in such a small country?

The vast military empire consists of 700 bases with some form of military personnel in 150 countries. Why do we need 179 U.S. military bases in Germany, 109 in Japan, 85 in South Korea, 58 in Italy, 37 in Puerto Rico and bases in 74 other countries? 1900 in Djibouti, 950 in Chad, 900 in Gabon, 2000 in Mali, 80 in Burkina Faso and troops in Senegal, Niger, Kosovo, Cameroon, Ivory Coast, Lebanon, Guinea, Honduras, Peru and in numerous other countries? And that's only a part of the entire network of bases and installations (*Payne 2015*).

The F35 fighter jet program initiated in 2001, has cost $396 billion to date. If continued to conclusion, it will end up costing over $1 trillion. And the worst part of it is that the development of this fighter jet has been plagued by a myriad of software/navigation problems, weapons delivery accuracy, flight control problems, reliability issues with avionics processors, landing gear issues, concerns with thermal management systems, ejection seat assembly issues, as well as problems with the cockpit display electronics unit, seat survival kits, igniter-spark in the turbine engines, and on-board oxygen generating systems.

While this country's national infrastructure worsens every day and would need at least $1 trillion to bring it up to acceptable levels, Congress has put this important need on the back burner because, for years, those funds have been earmarked for use in other countries where our military has been in action. $109 billion was spent in Afghanistan on its infrastructure and additionally, $60 billion was squandered in reconstruction in Iraq.

Several hundred billion dollars have been spent on the construction of over 500 military bases in both Iraq and Afghanistan, almost all of which are now either in the hands of those governments or under the control of terrorist factions. Military equipment that cost billions was left in Iraq when U.S. troops pulled out and ISIS gladly accepted this gift from the U.S. government which they proceeded to use to good advantage in Iraq and Syria.

- In 2004, when nearly $12 billion in $100 bills was flown into Iraq in huge cargo planes, what has been called biggest transfer of cash in the history of the Federal Reserve took place and then, it just seemed to disappear. It supposedly was intended to be distributed among Iraqi ministers and U.S. contractors but after numerous investigations, it was never determined who the actual end recipients were.

While all these pork-barrel type projects represent a monumental waste of taxpayer dollars, they have consistently been a great boon to the defense industry and to various civilian and military contractors. Their return on investment (ROI) has been fabulous while the ROI of the American people has been ZERO! Kind of like a Ponzi scheme, a scam investment *designed to separate investors (in this case, the American people) from their money.*

We badly need to unravel our twisted priorities. It is imperative that America be strong and stable domestically if we wish to continue to maintain a powerful, effective military. To do so, we must have a strong domestic foundation, which includes: a strong society, economy, infrastructure, system of education, adequately funded research and development, and health care to list just a few. That has not been happening as we pour massive amounts into the military and have little left for our important domestic needs.

One of this country's most effective forms of socialism, the U.S. military, provides safety and security for its people by guarding them from attacks by foreign enemies. Then when Americans retire, they receive Social Security and, if they so choose, they can join Medicare. So we can conclude that America's form of socialism is alive and well and dwells among us. Now why exactly should there exist this fear of socialism?

## The Invisible Government

Many view the prevailing political system in the U.S. today as being a polyarchy, which is a system where a small group (**1% Elite**) actually rules on behalf of capital, and the majority's (**99%**) decision making is confined to choosing among selective number of elites within a tightly controlled elective process. It is a form of consensual domination made possible by the structural domination of the global capital which allows for a concentration of political powers. Polyarchy and its procedures by itself may be insufficient for achieving full democracy. For example, poor people may be unable to participate in the political process. It is thought so, because some see *polyarchy* as a form of government that is not intended for greater social justice and cultural realization and to allow the repressed to politically participate. The unassuming general public is deceived into believing that their newly elected candidate will be the next great savior, until they realize four to eight years later that he or she was nothing more than another Musical Chairman controlled by the directives of the Invisible Government.

Others describe this biased political structure as a Plutocracy which in its simplest terms means a country or society ruled by the wealthy. This is also known as socialism for the rich. This particular political structure has very distinct attributes. Economic inequality is high. Social mobility is low, and workers struggle to climb out of poverty or capitalism for the poor. This describes the current U.S. system and the majority of the developed world societies today.

- Animals, due to their limited ability to think, prey upon one another physically through instinct.

- Humans, through their superior sense of intuition and capacity to think, prey upon one another financially.

## *End of Capitalism*

All a great power has to do to destroy itself is persist in trying to do the impossible. At the end of every Empire, which normally lasts about 250 years, everyone is out searching for the best of everything. But, you can never get enough of what you don't need. This is Capitalism's lifeline.

You can't have an effective Economic System where fewer and fewer people participate. U.S. CAPITALISM IS DESTROYING ITSELF.

- History has shown us that unrighteous ambition is at the Root of every Empire's demise – "But for those who are self-seeking and reject the truth and follow evil, there will be wrath and anger"(Romans 2:8 N.I.V.).

## *How do we fix this? Taxes? Public ownership of the means of production?*

First, we must begin to understand the complex nature of our current socioeconomic structure in the U.S. today.

Aside from the various social equality laws to include the Emancipation Proclamation, Civil Rights Act, Voter's Rights Act devised to eradicate racial inequality in this Country, we first must endeavor to understand the historical, political, and economic structure that governs 99% of us all.

*"Only traveling to places known, leads to a road going nowhere."*

# Chapter 7

# The Past is the Gateway to the Future

*"He who controls the Past – controls the Future" (George Orwell).*

## U.S. Economic Policy History

**THE CURRENT U.S. POLITICAL AND ECONOMIC SYSTEM** is an integrated structure based on Neoclassical Economic Theory. Our Founding Fathers envisioned a fully Democratic Society that protected the Rights and Liberties of All Citizens and supported a classical school of economic thought which stresses that economies function most efficiently if everyone is allowed to pursue his or her self-interest in an environment of free and open competition.

Traditionally, we've always been taxed on what we produce. The Founding Father's never intended for Americans to be taxed on Income and Labor. Taxation was originally based on land taxation and the unearned income, i.e. rental income which extends to natural resources in those lands. This form of taxation forced efficiency and eliminated the need for income taxes, sales taxes, and business taxes. Man-Made Capital has replaced more and more Natural Capital. Our self-interested economic system continues to deteriorate the more we continue to plunder our national capital. Material success has created social failure because the Growth (Capitalistic) Society demands that we make consumption a way of life.

In 1862, President Lincoln signed into law a revenue-raising measure to help pay for Civil War expenses. The measure created a Commissioner of Internal Revenue and the nation's first income tax. It levied a 3% tax on incomes between $600 and $10,000 and a 5% tax on incomes of more than $10,000. At the end of the Civil war in 1865, President Lincoln's income tax law expired and beginning in 1867, various proposals and laws were enacted unsuccessfully to revisit the necessity for income tax. As a result, the Internal Revenue Service was formulated in 1894 with limited authority to tax all U.S. citizens due to restrictive existing State laws. Finally, in 1913, Congress passed the sixteenth amendment giving the Internal Revenue Service full authority to tax every U.S. Citizen regardless of state population laws. This particular tax system was imported from British colonialism and has since duped the world.

Ironically, the Federal Reserve, the U.S. Central Bank was born as a result of the Panic of 1907, the worst U.S. recession to date. Most banks became insolvent. This prompted JP Morgan, the most powerful banker in the U.S., and five of his richest worldly friends to embark upon Jekyll Island, Georgia, for a secret meeting to discuss U.S. Banking and monetary reform. This meeting was known as The Creature of Jekyll Island. As a result, the Federal Reserve Central Bank, comprised of twelve Central banks nationwide, was finally formulated in 1913.

The idea for a U.S. Central Bank was brilliant, but the formation was grossly flawed in that the Federal Reserve literally is not a Federal Bank. It is controlled by private stockholders who happen to be from the same elitist families and heirs of the original founders. The Federal Reserve is privately owned; its shareholders are private banks. Our government essentially borrows from these privately controlled Central Banks with interest which obligates every U.S. Citizens to be responsible for the repayment accordingly. These are the same elitist power brokers who financially back and select political candidates which results in successful lobbying of favorable capitalistic laws.

## Birth of Fiat Money

The **Fiat System** of **Man-Made-Money** is based on man's law, not God's law. Gold is a natural form of money (God's way), and was the U.S. standard until 1971. To achieve human liberty, you really need to have sound money and Gold is the most effective way to accomplish this because **Gold is outside the control of politicians.**"

## *WHAT IS THE GOLD STANDARD?*

It's a monetary system that directly links a currency's value to that of gold. A country on the gold standard cannot increase the amount of money in circulation without also increasing its gold reserves. Because the global gold supply grows slowly, being on the gold standard would theoretically hold government overspending and inflation in check. No country currently backs its currency with gold.

## WHY DID THE U.S. ABANDON THE GOLD STANDARD?

**The U.S. abandoned its gold standard to help combat the Great Depression**. Faced with mounting unemployment and spiraling deflation in the early 1930s, the U.S. government found it could do little to stimulate the economy. To deter people from cashing in deposits and depleting the gold supply, the U.S. and other governments had to keep interest rates high, but that made it too expensive for people and businesses to borrow. So, in **1933, President Franklin D. Roosevelt cut the dollar's ties with gold** allowing the government to pump money into the economy and lower interest rates. "Most economists now agree ninety percent of the reason why the U.S. got out of the Great Depression was the break with gold," said Liaquat Ahamed, author of the book *Lords of Finance*. The U.S. continued to allow foreign governments to exchange dollars for gold until 1971, when President Richard Nixon abruptly ended the practice to stop dollar-flush foreigners from sapping U.S. gold reserves.

## WHY IS GOLD IN DEBATE AGAIN?

Libertarian Representative Ron Paul (R-Texas) made a return to honest money a key plank of his presidential run, and the idea took hold among Tea Party conservatives outraged over the Federal Reserve's loose monetary policies since the financial crisis. They argue that the U.S. debt now exceeds $18.92 trillion because the government has become too cavalier about borrowing and printing money. When the Fed prints money, gold-standard advocates say, it cheapens the value of the dollar, promotes inflation, and effectively steals money from the citizenry. The Republican Party's 2012 platform called for the creation of a commission to investigate setting a fixed value for the dollar. Think of it as a person with a debit card rather than a credit card. The debit card holder can only spend what he or she has in the bank.

## *Two Misconceptions about the Gold Standard:*

According to a recent article published by *Philosophical Economics*, two major misconceptions regarding the Gold Standard are explained.

The **first misconception** relates to the idea that the gold standard somehow caused or exacerbated the **Great Depression.** This simply is *not* true. What caused and exacerbated the Great Depression, from the Panic of 1930 until FDR's banking holiday in the spring of 1933, was the unwillingness on the part of the Federal Reserve to lend to solvent but illiquid banks.

The Fed's refusal to lend to banks facing runs had *nothing* to do with any constraint associated with the gold standard. Indeed, the Fed at the time was *flush* with gold. It held a gold reserve quantity equal to a near record 80% of the outstanding base money it had created.

 **The risk** that an economically illiterate public might panic and seek to redeem gold in numbers that exceed what the central bank has on **hand is the only risk a central bank ever really faces on a gold standard,** i.e. **The Great Recession Panic of 1907.**

The **second misconception** pertains to the idea that the US. f inancial system was somehow on a gold standard after 1933. It was not. The gold standard ended in the Spring of 1933, when FDR issued **executive order 6102**.

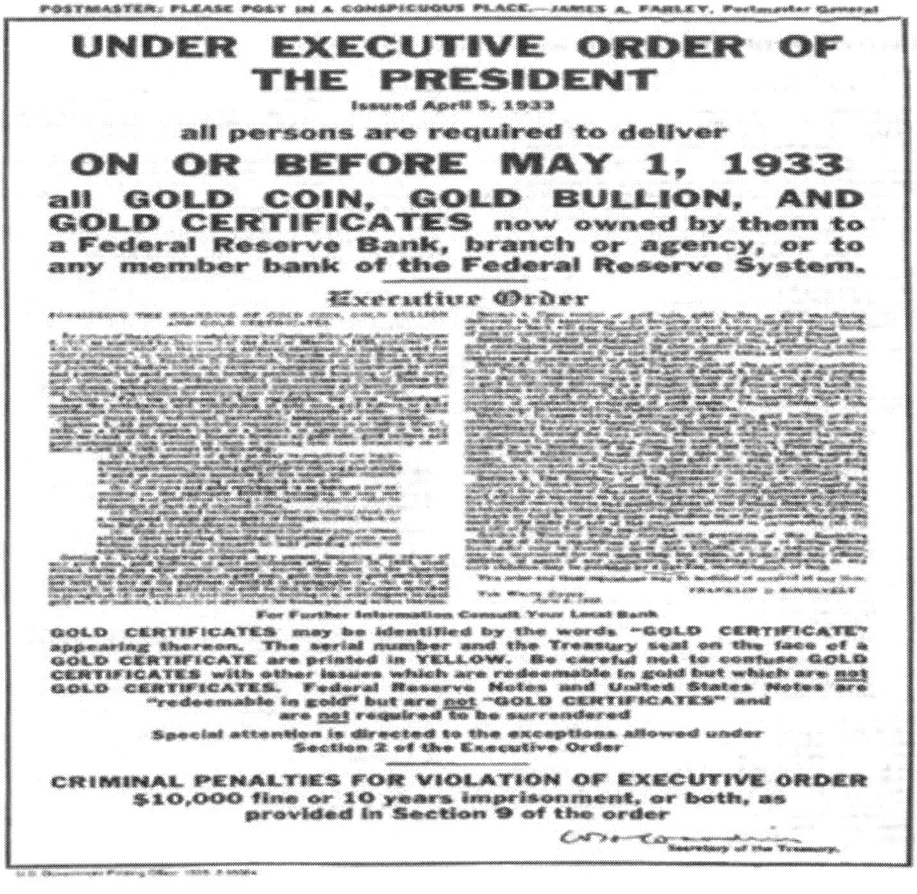

POSTMASTER: PLEASE POST IN A CONSPICUOUS PLACE.—JAMES A. FARLEY, Postmaster General

# UNDER EXECUTIVE ORDER OF THE PRESIDENT

Issued April 5, 1933

all persons are required to deliver

## ON OR BEFORE MAY 1, 1933

**all GOLD COIN, GOLD BULLION, AND GOLD CERTIFICATES now owned by them to a Federal Reserve Bank, branch or agency, or to any member bank of the Federal Reserve System.**

Executive Order

For Further Information Consult Your Local Bank

GOLD CERTIFICATES may be identified by the words "GOLD CERTIFICATE" appearing thereon. The serial number and the Treasury seal on the face of a GOLD CERTIFICATE are printed in YELLOW. Be careful not to confuse GOLD CERTIFICATES with other issues which are redeemable in gold but which are not GOLD CERTIFICATES. Federal Reserve Notes and United States Notes are "redeemable in gold" but are not "GOLD CERTIFICATES" and are not required to be surrendered

Special attention is directed to the exceptions allowed under Section 2 of the Executive Order

**CRIMINAL PENALTIES FOR VIOLATION OF EXECUTIVE ORDER**
**$10,000 fine or 10 years imprisonment, or both, as provided in Section 9 of the order**

Secretary of the Treasury.

This order made it illegal for individuals within the continental United States to own gold. If gold can't be legally owned, then it can't be legally redeemed. If it can't be legally redeemed, then it can't constrain the central bank.

The gold standard that was in place from the mid-1930s until 1971 was *figurative* and *ceremonial* in nature. The Fed's gold, which backed the dollar, could not be redeemed by the public, therefore the backing had no bite.

To be clear, on a fiat monetary system, the market retains the ability to put the central bank in check. Instead of redeeming money directly from the central bank in gold, market participants can redeem money by refusing to hold it, choosing instead to hold assets that they think will retain value such as land, durables, precious metals, foreign currencies, foreign securities, foreign real estate, etc. If such an occurrence were to happen enmasse, and if there is a concomitant monetary expansion taking place alongside it, the result will be uncontrolled inflation. The probability that such a rejection will occur is obviously much less on a fiat system, where the option of old redemption isn't there to tempt things. But the theoretical power to reject the money as money, which is what the idea of gold redemption formalizes, is still there.

## Conclusion

The reason not to use monetary systems based on gold is that they are obsolete and unnecessary with no real benefits over fiat systems, but with many inconveniences and disadvantages. In a fiat system, the central bank can create base money in whatever amount would be *economically appropriate* to create. But on a gold-based system, the central bank is forced to create whatever amount of base money the mining industry can mine, and to destroy whatever amount of base money a panicky public wants destroyed. If the goal is to constrain the central bank, then constrain it directly with laws. Put a legal limit on how much money it can issue or on what it can purchase. Alternatively, if you are a developing country that does not enjoy the confidence of the market, peg your currency to the currency of a country that does enjoy that confidence.

# A Fiat Nation

## *Fiat Money and a Sovereign Democracy*

According to an article posted in the *New Economic Perspective* by Devin Smith who referenced excerpts from the very respected works of Pulitzer Prize winner, Edward O. Wilson's book, *The Social Conquest of Earth*. The book takes an in-depth look at what happens when a Sovereign Power becomes a Democracy?

This is essentially the problem the U.S. confronted in 1971. The solution was quite simple. The U.S. abandoned the gold standard and declared the U.S. dollar would no longer be convertible to anything other than itself. The U.S. dollar returned to the original pure fiat money valuation. What DID NOT change, however, was the system that had been set up to protect the back-up gold supply. By law, the U.S. sovereign government *continued* to sell treasury bonds to citizens in order to get the fiat dollars it needed in order to spend MORE each year than it collected in taxes. And the citizens continued to benefit from this ingenious bargain. They continued to exchange their saved fiat dollars for sovereign treasury bonds that paid interest. *And,* they continued to add to their savings—and build their private economy—as the sovereign government continued to spend MORE each year than it collected in taxes.

## *The dangers of Fiat Money and Democracy*

The fact that the Democracy did not vote to change the law when the gold-standard was abandoned has created today the confused perception that a great problem exists for which there is no reasonable solution. The problem is this: As the sovereign government continues to sell Treasury bonds to get the fiat dollars it needs to spend MORE than it collects in taxes, the interest it will be paying the citizens holding the bonds will become a larger and larger component of annual sovereign spending requiring the sovereign government to sell even *more* Treasury bonds to make up the difference. It is unlikely that the bonds will be owned equally amongst the citizens, but rather will be held by an elite group of financiers' who will become fabulously wealthy, but the sovereign government itself will *appear* to have fallen hopelessly into debt.

This leads us to put into proper context, the current state of U.S. fiscal affairs as it relates to Gross Domestic Product (GDP) and National Debt:

## *U.S. Gross Domestic Product:*

GDP is the total market value of all final goods and services produced in a country in a given year.

The United States is the largest economy in the world at nominal exchange rate basis. The nominal exchange rate is defined as the number of units of the domestic currency that can purchase a unit of a given foreign currency; the US dollar is the World Standard Currency. With a 2015 economy of around $18.06 trillion, the United States holds a 22.53% share of global GDP in nominal terms. The GDP of the United States is $703.9 billion more than second ranked China. China contributes 13.43% of the total world economic output. Despite losing $303 billion in 2014, Japan is still at number three. United States and China contributes 35.96% of the world's GDP. The top three countries contribute 41.93% of world's GDP.

The United States has one of the most diversified and most technologically advanced economies in the world. Finance, insurance, real estate, rental, leasing, health care, social assistance, professional, business and educational services account for more than 40% of GDP. Retail and wholesale trade creates another 12% of the wealth. The government related services fuel 13% of GDP. Utilities, transportation and warehousing and information account for 10% of the GDP. Manufacturing, mining, and construction constitute 17% of the output.

- The U.S. has maintained itself as the world's largest economic society since the 1890's when such wealth was largely generated as a direct result of 400 years of indentured servitude and slave labor.

The Gross Domestic Product in the United States expanded an annualized 2.10% in 2015. The United States averaged 3.26% from 1947 until 2014, reaching an all-time high of 16.90% in the first quarter of 1950 and a record low of -10% in the first quarter of 1958. However, in spite of successfully maintaining our number one ranking of being the world's most economically productive society with a current 2015 GDP of $18.06 trillion. When you dig deeper, understanding that the U.S. also has an alarming public national debt of $18.92 trillion,this simply means that our National Debt to GDP ratio represents 105% (our national debt exceeds GDP by − 5% or $860 billion)) and represents the second highest in U.S. history. This ratio further represents a net increase of $640 billion from 2014, when the ratio was 102.20%, then the third highest in U.S. history. The National Debt has continued to outpace the GDP since 2013. Also, as a frame of reference, U.S. Debt to GDP ratio only averaged 60.81% from 1940 until 2012, with a record high of 121.7% in 1946 immediately following the Great Depression, and a low of 31.70% in 1974.

*Furthermore, 70% of total U.S. GDP output in 2015 was generated from consumer spending which confirms our theorem that with the continued elimination of middle income wage earners and stagnant wages overall -*

*"U.S. Capitalism is headed for dissolution."*

## *National Debt:*
In 2015, the National Debt is a staggering $18.92 trillion and growing beyond control.The current U.S. business model is undeniably broken and unless a new plan is devised, we are headed towards insolvency.

• In 1995, the Federal deficit was $4.97 trillion and has steadily increased over the last 20 years to an astounding $18.92 trillion in 2015. This is a whopping 3,807% increase and growing. Actually, from 1950 through 1993, the U.S. debt also increased but at a much reasonably slower pace.

The majority of the $18.92 trillion in U.S. Government debt is backed or guaranteed by U.S.Treasury Bonds, the root of the word bondage. Debt enslaves us and future generations. With a total of only 122 million full-time U.S. employees in 2015 (unadjusted), we are equally indebted to the Government for approximately $154,161 each; 2014 interest payments alone paid by taxpayers on this debt totaled $229 billion.

According to a recent insightful article in *Forbes* by Mike Patton, the following findings are disclosed:

## *Owners of U.S.A. Debt:*

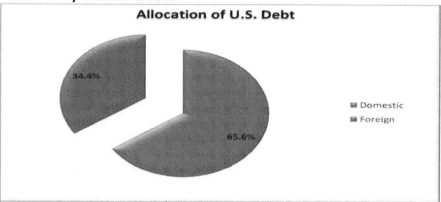

**Allocation of U.S. Debt**

34.4%

65.6%

■ Domestic
■ Foreign

The largest owner of U.S. debt is Social Security. Since the Social Security system is a government entity, how can the government own its own debt? Good question. This is where the house of cards theory resides. Some believe the federal government is merely moving the IOUs from one shell to another, hoping to escape the watchful eye of its citizens. In any event, Social Security owns about 16% of the debt followed by other federal government entities (13%), and the Federal Reserve (12%). How much is owned by foreign governments? The following chart contains the answer.

According to the U.S. Treasury Department, at the end of August 2014, more than a third of the debt was owned by foreign countries (34.4%). The largest foreign holders of U.S. debt were Mainland China (7.2%) and Japan (7.0%). What is the consequence of having such a large percentage of debt held by foreign nations? It depends. It depends on the relationship between the U.S. and the specific foreign country. It also depends on the global interest rate environment. Finally, it depends on the geo-political climate and the degree of fear around the globe. This is the case because when fear rises money flows into U.S. Treasuries which is viewed as a safe place to invest. The percentage of debt owned by countries that are less friendly to America is about 10%. This includes China, several oil exporters (Ecuador, Venezuela, Iran, Iraq, Libya, etc.), and a few others. The worst case scenario would materialize if the largest holders decided to sell their Treasury securities at the same time. This could potentially decrease demand which would push yields higher. If yields rose, the Federal Government would find it more difficult to service the debt, pushing the deficit higher. If the deficit rose, the total debt burden would accelerate, and unless demand for U.S. debt was to increase, it could get ugly. Will this transpire? It's not too likely in the foreseeable future.

## *Conclusion*

Given the state of the global markets, the U.S. is still considered to be the best house in a bad neighborhood. Even though more than one third of the debt is owned by foreign nations, as long as there are no safer places to invest, money will find its way here. Therefore, global turmoil would be in the best interest of the federal government. Anything which raises fear will bring money to the Treasury and allay the need for higher taxes.

## *Trending Red Alert:*

Foreign Country's have been divesting their respective holding of U.S. Treasury Bonds to the tune of $56 billion during the months of January/February 2015...

• The nation's deficit is, in *actuality,* a balance-sheet account of the fiat money the sovereign has spent into the private economy but not collected back in taxes.

• As long as there is work that can be done to improve the lives and well-being of the citizens, and as long as the labor and sustainable resources are available to accomplish that work in exchange for sovereign fiat dollars, the Sovereign Nation *can afford* to have the work accomplished and therefore has the capacity to service the debt.

The strange reality of fiat money tells us the only limitations we *actually* have are the natural and physical resources available - our ability to cooperate, and our willingness to confront and constrain any elite group that seeks to take control of and manipulate sovereign spending and taxing for the purpose of self-enrichment and power.

• Today, a powerful elite group does control the majority of private U.S. Treasuries.

• Today, the U.S. Sovereign Nation cannot afford to accomplish its work.

## *Here's Why:*

In the U.S. today, our natural resources are severally depleted, physical resources are severely underutilized as evidenced by a 62.6% workforce participation rate,an eroding Middle-Class tax base, tax-dodging Corporations, and a declining education system. Our refusal to cooperate due to xenophobic delusion, and our collective delusion to not confront and constrain the capitalistic elite groups, places great limitations on the U.S. economy's ability to sustain our current Fiat Money System going forward, total collapse is imminent.

This leads me to borrow a quote from our sixteenth president, *Abraham Lincoln*:

* "No generations have the right to contract debts greater than can be paid off during the course of its own existence."

A generation is normally defined as the difference in age of years between the birth of children and parents, and on average equates to 20 to 30 years.

A true nation exists when all the people of the land share the profits TOGETHER. **We currently only share in the debts together.**

## The Dollar Dilemma:

*Used to say* – "This Note is Legal Tender for all debts public and private, and is "redeemable" in lawful money at the US Treasury and any Federal Reserve Bank.

*Now says* – This Note is legal tender for all debts public and private; changed in 1963, when the promises of "redemption" vanished from the face of each note.

Note defined – A written promise to pay; therefore U.S. dollar represents an IOU against current and future labor production.

Note = Debt (these Federal Reserve "Notes" now have no value for themselves because they are "Not Redeemable" in Gold, Silver or any other commodity and are only backed by U.S. GDP.

Insight: 2015 US GDP to Debt ratio was 1.05% which = (-0.05%) negative growth, therefore the U.S. $ has $0 Intrinsic Value...."coercive trust drives consumer confidence" – therefore Government spending is the only thing "Backing the U.S. $ dollar; taxes and printing Fiat Money.

*"The relative value of money is limited to the confidence of the beholder."*

## Case in Point:

When I was an eight year old 3rd grader, we went on a Bank Field trip whereby I remember asking the Branch Manager the distinct question being – "How does a Bank run out of Money…can't they just print more? She was totally stunned and not only could she not answer my question, no other bank Officers could either.

Mind you, this was around 1968, during a time when the U.S. dollar, although not totally backed by a "Gold Reserve" which was abandoned in 1931, the US Dollar remained tied to the Gold Standard until 1971 when President Nixon abandoned all ties to the US Dollar and Gold, therefore, in 1968 it was "prohibitive" for the Federal Reserve to simply print "Fiat Money" out of thin air as they practice today.

## U.S. Debt Paradox:

According to **James Dale Davidson** (Well endowed Economist) May 2016 Article – **2016 Economic Collapse/Elimination of Social Security** (Forbes/Barron's and others concurred):

The U.S. Economic Foundation is broken due to excessive debt versus viable productivity:

- The Federal Reserve has purchased 70% of its own Treasury Bonds since 2009 (Past Years 10 – 15%)

- 2015 National Debt was $18.92 trillion; exceeding GDP by 5% or $1 trillion

- U.S. Total Indebtedness (Fiscal Gap); $210 trillion (current Debt $18.92 trillion + Future Social Entitlements $190.08 trillion).

*My Theory Proven*: With a declining "Labor Base"; spending will continue to outpace GDP – further "Debasing" the economy…U.S. dollar.

Thus, I render this verdict. The U.S. will experience a future financial crisis on a level not seen in this country since 1946.

## New Government Game Plan – BAIL-IN

### *MyRA (My Retirement Account)*
According a trending *TEA PARTY.org* article published on February 14, 2014, "Obamanomics."

(Info Wars) – This morning Reuters obtained a leaked proposal disclosing that European Union officials are looking for new and innovative ways to fund their immense debt levels.

As noted by Zero Hedge, they're no longer turning exclusively to central bankers to simply print more money as needed. Because last year's bank bail-in forcing the confiscation of funds from average depositors in Cyprus worked so well, EU regulators and bankers have determined that they'll use a similar method to fund their future endeavors.

In a nutshell, and in Reuters' own words, the savings of the European Union's 500 million citizens could be used to fund long-term investments to boost the economy and help plug the gap left by banks since the financial crisis, an EU document says.

The solution? The Commission will ask the bloc's insurance watchdog in the second half of this year for advice on a possible draft law to mobilize more personal pension savings for long-term financing, the document said.

This is basically the offer that President Obama of the United States floated last night.

- And like an undiscerning used car salesman, he actually pitched Americans on loaning their retirement savings to the U.S. government with a straight face, guaranteeing a decent return with no risk of losing what you put in.

- This is his new MyRA program. And the aim is simple, dupe unwitting Americans to plow their retirement savings into the U.S. government's shrinking coffers.

The government is flat breaking. Even by their own assessment, the U.S. government's national debt in 2015 was $18.92 trillion.

Here's the thing: according to the IRS, there is well over $5 trillion in U.S. individual retirement accounts. For a government as bankrupt as Uncle Sam is, $5 trillion is irresistible.

They need that money. They need YOUR money. And this MyRA program is the critical first step to corralling your hard earned retirement funds.

A few years ago the government of the United States of America nationalized nearly 1/6th of our economy when they took over the Health Care System (Obamacare) with forced mandates. In the process, they essentially took control of $1.6 trillion in yearly industry revenues.

But that's nothing compared to private savings. The total amount of retirement assets in America, including 401k, IRA and savings accounts is around $21 trillion. With our national debt coincidentally approaching the same, the government sees big money and a potential way out of our country's fiscal disaster.

This will start voluntarily with the MyRA and other state-sponsored programs. But when not enough Americans are making it their patriotic duty to turn over their funds to their government, they'll mandate compliance with the stroke of a pen just as they did with the *Patient Affordable Care Act*.

And just like Obamacare, it will be enforced by the barrel of a gun. Failure to comply will mean confiscation without recourse and prison time.

- The U.S. Government successfully launched the MyRA Program on November 4, 2014. No major advertising was done purposely to stay under the radar of popular media. Watch out!

## Capital Currency Controls:

There appears to be an unprecedented U.S. currency policy going into effect and we all need to take notice with keen attentiveness according to a recent Forecasts & Trends E-Letter by Gary D. Halbert, published on May 6, 2014, *Are Currency Controls also known as Capital Controls Coming to America July 1, 2014?*

## *Overview*

Some very controversial regulations passed way back in 2010 and finalized in 2012 are scheduled to go into effect, and most Americans know little or nothing about this new law. Yet the effect of these new regulations could send shock waves through the financial system worldwide. Basically, the regulations that take effect will make it very difficult and costly for Americans to hold money or investments outside the U.S.

Starting in July, foreign banks and financial institutions will be required to report to the IRS any accounts they hold which are owned by Americans, including the owner's name, address, Tax ID number (or Social Security number) and account balances of all offshore accounts if the combined amount is over $50,000. Many foreign institutions are up in arms about this, and some are kicking their U.S. clients out to avoid reporting this information to the IRS. Most U.S. investors who have money in offshore banks, funds, etc. will very likely close such accounts and bring their money home when they learn about this.

The Democrats who passed this law back in 2010 when they controlled Congress say these new regulations were designed simply to identify tax cheats who do not pay the IRS taxes on their gains earned outside the U.S. But the unintended consequence may be a major disruption in the global financial system that could cause the U.S. dollar to plunge. Some even believe it could threaten the U.S. dollar's status as the world's Reserve Currency.

- Some analysts are calling the new law *Currency Controls also known as Capital Controls,* which have never happened before in the U.S.

**First, any announcement will probably not use the words *capital controls*.** It will be couched positively, for the greater good, and words like patriotic duty will likely feature prominently in mainstream press and government press releases. If you try to transfer assets outside your country, you could be branded as a traitor or an enemy of the state, even among some in your own social circles.

## The Foreign Account Tax Compliance Act

In 2010, the then Democrat-controlled Congress passed the **Foreign Account Tax Compliance Act** (FATCA). At the time, supporters said the new law was designed to ensure that U.S. citizens banking and/or investing internationally could not avoid paying taxes on their income from offshore accounts and assets. In essence, it is a program aimed at uncovering undeclared income hidden by Americans in banks, funds, etc. around the world.

The premise of FATCA seems relatively simple: identify account holders and the dollar value of each account they hold in foreign banks, other financial institutions, offshore funds, etc. if it is **over $50,000** collectively. That's not hard, right? Well, it depends.

### *FATCA Applies to All U.S. Persons:*
The term United States Person means:

- A U.S. citizen (including dual citizen)
- A U.S. resident alien for tax purposes
- A domestic partnership
- A domestic corporation
- Any estate other than a foreign estate
- Any trust if:
    1. A court within the United States is able to exercise primary supervision over the administration of the trust, and
    2. One or more United States persons have the authority to control all substantial decisions of the trust
    3. Any other person that is not a foreign person.

- **FATCA** relies on partner nations (like **Britain, Germany, France, Italy, Spain** and many others) and other information pathways to discover both the identity of American foreign account holders and the taxable amount in those same accounts.

- Any foreign entity making a payment (interest, dividends, capital gains, etc.) **to American-owned accounts** must consider whether it is subject to FATCA. And FATCA may apply to both financial and non-financial operating companies abroad. U.S. banks and financial institutions must reciprocate by providing the same information to foreign regulators for any of their citizens who have accounts in the U.S.!

**Starting July 1, 2015, Foreign Financial Institutions (FFIs)** will have to start providing the IRS with the personal income information listed above on an annual basis. But that's just the beginning. Starting on January 1, 2015, FATCA will require FFIs to actually withdraw (**withhold**) **30%** of any yearly gains in Americans' foreign accounts and submit that to the IRS each year. American entities that make payments to foreigners who have accounts in the U.S. will also be impacted as they will soon be required to withhold a portion of any income paid to non-U.S. persons under FATCA.

Simply put, the Obama Administration and the Liberal Democrats in Congress do not want Americans investing abroad, and it is requiring foreign financial institutions to enforce its policy.

## *Why FATCA Could Be Bearish for the U.S. Dollar:*

Since the U.S. Dollar is the world's Reserve Currency, most FFI's hold significant reserves of dollars, while most FFI's have reluctantly agreed to FATCA, they are very likely to re-examine how much business they will continue to do in U.S. Dollar transactions. Already we are seeing China, Russia, Brazil, India, South Africa and other countries moving away from using the U.S. Dollar in trade with each other and with other nations.

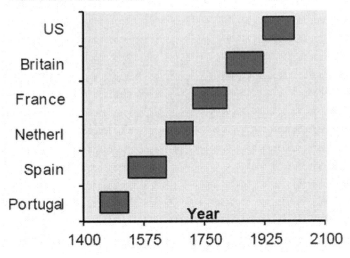

## (c37) Reserve currency status does not last forever

- I do believe that the U.S. Dollar is destined to be replaced as the Reserve currency at some point in the future due to our exploding National Debt and dangerous policies such as FATCA.

### *IRS Delays FATCA Enforcement:*

In Notice 2014-33, the IRS announced that calendar years 2014 and 2015 would be regarded as a transition period for the purpose of IRS enforcement.

### *Conclusion*

At the end of the day, **FATCA** is just another **money grab** by the politicians in Washington. They know that the law will, in effect, prohibit investing in offshore accounts. They may as well call it **Currency Controls.**

What they apparently don't know is that FATCA will be bearish for the U.S. dollar and may eventually threaten its status as the world's reserve currency. Or maybe they do know.

**Monetary Shift**: More importantly, the advancement of Bitcoin and more specifically Blockchain Technology, the reliance on a World Reserve Currency has been further diminished and will continue as these technologies advance respectively and here's why:

# The Arrival of Bitcoin

Bitcoin was developed in 2009 as a crypto-currency, i.e. "Digital Gold"

- Like Gold – there is a finite supply of Bitcoin (maximum production is 21 million by 2140).

- Like Gold – and everything else – humans attach value to all things over time.

*Any economic item is only worth what someone is willing to pay for it at a given time.

## *Advantages over Gold:*
- Uncheatable – Predictable – Scheduled
- Bitcoin is a more transportable version of Gold and unlike Gold; has infinite divisibility (can be purchased in any denomination out to 8 decimal points).
- Bitcoin is backed by time; (mined every 10 minutes by automated algorithums).
- Requires no Central Banking Authority.
- Requires no currency exchange – Universal currency.
- Currently 40% of World's Population is "Unbanked" – Bitcoin serves as a "Bridge."
- Fees are lowest of any other "Money Service Provider" – less than 1% per transaction.
- All transactions can be completed using a "Smart Phone" – 85% of World's population.
- Retail Merchants benefit from a cash transaction (no charge backs).

## *Global Reserve Relevance: The universal construct of time is the "Backing" of Bitcoin.*
**Blockchain,** the technology underlying the digital currency **Bitcoin,** has sparked intense interest across industries from **banking** and **trading** to **agriculture** and **music.** Large-scale deployment of the technology, a digital ledger of industries and transactions, could be years away. Yet the level of commitment to testing and development, especially in financial services, shows how seriously blockchain is viewed in the corporate world.

The **power** of **blockchain** lies, advocates say, ***in its inherent security,*** which can establish trust directly among parties in a transaction, making it possible to remove the middlemen that currently serve that function. Entire industries, such as clearinghouses in financial trading or title-search firms in real estate, conceivably could be **displaced,** slashing costs and cutting the time required to complete a transaction. The impact, they say, could be massive.

In the long run, digital currencies will not only ***help bootstrap financial services in places like Nigeria,*** but ***remake money systems elsewhere in the world.*** It may start in the near to mid-term going mainstream in some of these emerging markets, but in the long term, that's a catalyst for it going mainstream in more developed places. Because it provides such an effective means of *tracking money* and *who holds that money* at any given time, it can streamline costs everywhere. *It's hard to imagine things working online in any other way than the way* bitcoin *does it.*

### ***Bitcoin represents the new Universal Monetary Equalizer***

# Chapter 8

# The Unbalanced Scales That Plague Us

*The unbalanced scales that plague us are the unjust and unequitable world capitalist systems aka **"Goliath's of the world"**; Inequitable Political, Social, and Economic Systems, Poverty, Homelessness, Food Insecurity, Racial persecution, Economic Inequality, Mass Incarceration, Voter Suppression, Unjust Criminal Justice System, Separate & Unequal Schools, Racial, Class, and Religious Discrimination.*

**THE ENTIRE U.S. NATION IS ONE BIG ECOSYSTEM** that is dependent on every member citizen's talents, gifts, input, participation, and production to function effectively, efficiently, and harmoniously. This is grossly out of balance today. Due to various societal and economic challenges to include Poverty, Crime, Unemployment, Underemployment, Inequality, Civil Unrest, Class Warfare, Immigration, Discrimination, Segregation, Dysfunctional Education System, Social Entitlement Instability, Religious Disorder, Out-of-Control Gun Laws, Unprecedented Violence, Untrustworthy Politicians, Corporate Inversions, Skyrocketing National Debt, War Escalations, and continuous *xenophobic practices* that continue to contribute to a substantially declining socioeconomic landscape in this once great Nation of ours.

## State of the Union:

In 2013, the U.S. government spent **$1 trillion or $21,700** per citizen on anti-poverty programs with minimum measurable results considering that 15% or **49 million citizens** remain in poverty and one out of three children live in poverty. An additional **$174 billion was spent** on college financial aid which has allowed most colleges to increase enrollments, however, their graduation rates have continually decreased.

Approximately 70% of students actually graduate taking an average of six years to complete a four-year degree while amassing an average of $30,000 in student loan debt. On a world-wide scale, the U.S. ranked only fourteenth has the most educated country. More politicians have been indicted for corruption nationwide in the past five years than any other time in recent history. Terrorist threats have continued to plague the U.S. over the last decade and have actually accelerated i.e. ISIS. Since the Civil Rights Act of 1964, Black Poverty, Crime, and Segregation is far worse due to more aggressive practices of *xenophobic behavior.* **Middle Class Wage Earners** have virtually been eliminated as a result of the 2009 Financial Crisis, and Corporate Inversions are at unprecedented levels in that more and more of the most profitable U.S. Corporations are diverting taxable profits overseas to avoid paying taxes which severely impacts the monetary stability of this Country.

If not brought under control in the immediate future, the U.S. as we know it will be on the verge of insolvency. Various economic studies further support the fact that among developed nations, the U.S. is the least economically and socially mobile country in the world. It is well documented that only 6% of U.S. children born at the bottom of the income ladder move up into the top fifth wealth percentile while almost 50% of them remain in the bottom. In contrast, 39% of children born in the top fifth stay at the top. Furthermore, American men born in the bottom fifth of family incomes have a 42% chance of staying there.

As you start to dig deeper, the major disparities and effects that poverty, inequality, and discrimination play against minorities in terms of Education, Unemployment/Underemployment, and incarceration is alarming.Black's represent just **13%** of the population but commit **59%** of the murders. Black overall crime rates are much worse today than they were before the Civil rights movements. Black men in their twenty's without a high school diploma are more likely today to be incarcerated than employed and nearly **70%** of middle-aged Black men who never graduated from high school have been incarcerated. Statistical data is just beginning to be compiled for Hispanics and other impoverished minorities. Currently, Blacks comprise 50% of the U.S. prison population while Hispanics comprise 30% (80% combined). This is not a **White-Black problem**. This is an **American Problem**.

## De facto Apartheid Nation:

Even when we venture further to evaluate minority High School and College Graduates, eventhough we have far less incarceration than their less educated incarcerated brethren, we continue to see high unemployment (National 7.1%, Minorities - Mostly Blacks/Hispanics 15%). The Black/White Income Gap is roughly 40% greater today than it was in 1967.This fact has led many National and International Economic Advisors to declare the U.S. as a de facto Apartheid Country and it is warranted.

## The Naked Truth

**This Urban Institute 2015 report** reveals just how little African-American and Hispanic families have in liquid retirement savings, particularly compared to White families. In 2013, the average White family had more than $130,000 in liquid retirement savings, compared to $19,000 for the average African-American family and $12,000 for the average Hispanic family.

Average Family Liquid Retirement Savings, 1989–2013

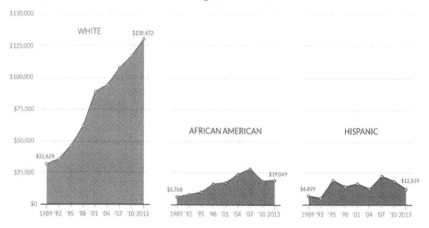

Source: Urban Institute calculations from Survey of Consumer Finances 1989-2013.

Notes: 2013 dollars. Liquid retirement savings include dollars in accounts such as 401(k), 403(b), and IRAs. Median liquid retirement savings for African American and Hispanic families were zero from 1989 to 2013. Median liquid retirement savings for whites were zero through the mid-1990s, about $1,500 in 1998, and $5,000 in 2013.

URBAN **INSTITUTE**

In some ways, **this understates the retirement crisis for everyone— African-American and Hispanic families, as well as Whites**. The Urban Institute also looked at liquid retirement savings for the median family, not the average. That's important because a few very rich people at the top of the income distribution can distort the statistics. Twenty people are in a bar, each of whom make $50,000 a year. Then Bill Gates walks into the bar. Suddenly, the average income of each person in the bar skyrockets. But that's just a result of Gates' exorbitant income, not everyone in the bar getting richer. **Using the median overcomes this problem**.

**"Median wealth shows how the typical person is doing,"** said Signe-Mary McKernan, one of the researchers behind the study. "If you line everybody up in order, you're just grabbing out that middle person and seeing how they are doing."

**And that's where the liquid retirement savings data is most alarming**. The median White family has just $5,000 in liquid retirement savings, up from $1,500 in 1998. For African-American and Hispanic families, the median is zero ($0.00).

Minority families have trouble saving for retirement for two other reasons outlined in the Urban Institute Study.

**First**, they have lower homeownership rates, which, while not a liquid savings vehicle, is one of the most common ways that Americans save. More than twenty percent of Americans over the age of 60 have savings in real estate or land. But the **homeownership rate for Whites is more than 50 percent larger than the rate for African-American and Hispanic families**—and the gap has stayed constant for the past thirty years.

Homeownership Rate by Race/Ethnicity, 1983-2013

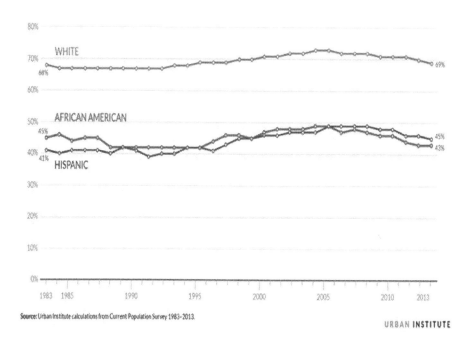

Source: Urban Institute calculations from Current Population Survey 1983-2013.

URBAN INSTITUTE

## *Urban Institute*

**Second, African-Americans families have more student loan debt than Whites**. In 2013, **42%** of African-American families had student loan debt, compared to just **28 %**of Whites and **16%** of Hispanics. And, as the Urban Institute authors note, African-Americans have lower graduation rates than Whites. People of color disproportionately attend **for-profit schools, which have low graduation rates**. That means **African-Americans aren't just taking on more debt, they also aren't always getting a degree for that debt.**

## Share of Families With Student Loan Debt for Those Ages 25-55, 1989-2013

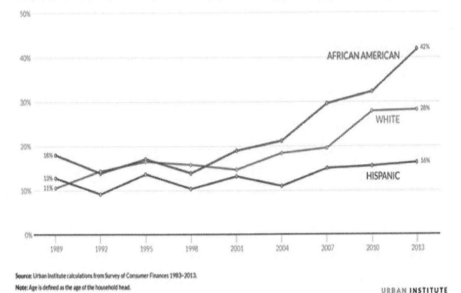

Source: Urban Institute calculations from Survey of Consumer Finances 1983-2013.
Note: Age is defined as the age of the household head.

URBAN **INSTITUTE**

A more current and direct analysis performed and disclosed by Thomas Shapiro in a 2013 Brandeis University Studyrevealed the following insights:

Brandeis researchers looked at a set of 1,700 families over the twenty-five-year period to see how their actual work and school experiences affected their wealth accumulation.

What they found is that home ownership is driving the growing gap. Price appreciation is more limited in non-White neighborhoods, making it harder for Blacks to build equity. Also, because Whites are more likely to have family financial assistance for down payments, they are able to buy homes an average of eight years earlier than Black families and put down larger upfront payments that lower interest rates and mortgage costs.

The home ownership rate for Whites is 28% higher than that of Blacks.

How housing wealth is created in different communities is clearly what is driving this.

**Income gains are also a major differentiating factor**, even when Whites and Blacks have similar wage increases. Whites are typically able to put more of their raises towards accumulating wealth because they've already built up a cash cushion. Blacks are more likely to use the money to cover emergencies.

Inheritances also make it easier for some families to build wealth. Among the families studied, Whites were five times more likely to inherit money than Blacks, and their typical inheritances were ten timeslarger in value.

When it comes to education, Black graduates are often more saddled with college loans, making it harder for them to start socking away savings than their White peers. 80% of Black students graduate with debt, compared to 64% of Whites.

Researchers have repeatedly found discrimination in the job market. When two nearly identical résumés are sent out, it has been documented that the candidate with a White-sounding name receives more callbacks than the applicant with a Black-sounding name.

Blacks and Latinos at all education levels, including college and advanced degrees, earn less than their White and Asian counterparts, which means lower lifetime earnings and less ability to save.

Another reason why the income and wealth ratios are highest among White and Asian college graduates is that they are more likely than Black or Hispanic college graduates to have graduate or professional degrees. Advanced degrees typically provide significantly higher earnings and are strongly associated with greater wealth accumulation.

"The growing Wealth Gap has wider ramifications, "Shapiro" said. "If the pattern continues, people could start believing the deck is stacked against them and lose Hope."

Sorry,but people have already lost hope, according to the dismal rate that only 48% of all eligible High Students enrolled in college in 2015.

Our economy cannot sustain its growth in the face of this type of extreme wealth inequality.

## U.S. Workforce:

In 2015, the total U.S. Fully Employed Workforce stands at 122 million and declining due in part by the Financial Crisis of 2009, Corporate Outsourcing, Corporate Inversions, low College graduation rates, unprepared College Graduates, displaced middle-income employees and an exploding baby boomer retiring population; 10,000 baby boomers are retiring per day which equates to *3.65 million baby boomers per year. This amounts to 76 million retirees in 18 years. Workforce participation in the U.S. currently stands at a mere 62.6%*, meaning that only 62.6% of the eligible U.S Workforce is actually working.

- Another way to look at this is the fact that 37.4% or approximately 73 million eligible U.S. Workers don't work. Actually, the figure is 94 million if you consider Part-Time jobs as well. These numbers are the worst they've been in thirty-seven years, since 1978. And, the net effect is that the shrinking workforce limits the U.S. ability to grow the economy, sustain the world's largest economy, and to maintain financial sufficiency.

## U.S. Minimum Wage Rate:

**Adjusted for inflation, the federal minimum wage peaked in 1968,** at **$8.54** (in 2014 dollars). Since it was last raised in 2009, to the current $7.25 per hour, the federal minimum has lost about 8.1% of its purchasing power to inflation. The Economist recently estimated that, given how rich the U.S. is and the pattern among other advanced economies in the Organization for Economic Cooperation and Development (OECD), one would expect America to pay a minimum wage around $12 per hour.

The Congressional Budget Office (CBO) estimated in 2014, that raising the minimum wage to $10.10 and indexing it to inflation would increase the wages of 16.5 million workers in 2016. Raising the minimum wage to $9.00 without indexing would affect 7.6 million workers. Among workers paid by the hour in 2013, 1.5 million were reported as earning exactly the prevailing federal minimum wage. About 1.8 million were reported as earning wages below the minimum. Together, these 3.3 million workers with wages at or below the minimum represent 2.5% of all workers and 4.3% of hourly workers.

According to a U.C. Berkeley study published in 2015, low-wage jobs cost taxpayers nearly $153 billion annually because of working families' dependence on public safety net programs. According to the analysis, half of public dollars spent on Medicaid, the Children's Health Insurance Program, Temporary Assistance for Needy Families, the Earned Income Tax Credit, and the Supplemental Nutrition Assistance Program goes toward supporting working—not unemployed—families. That's basically the entire federal social safety net.

McDonald's alone costs tax payers $1.2 billion annually owing to workers enrolled in public assistance programs, according to a 2013 study from the National Employment Law Project.

Higher wages could help to reduce the burden on government programs, but the maximum annual earnings for a person working for $15 an hour—eight hours a day, Monday through Friday, every week of the yearonly amounts to $30,600, or about 20 % above the federal poverty level for a family of four. In California, eligibility for CalFresh, the state's food stamps program, is cut off when a household's gross earnings exceed 200 % of the poverty level. In other words, earning the gold standard wage of the fight for $15 movement doesn't necessarily mean you can get off of public assistance. According to the Berkeley study, 10.3 million working families were enrolled in SNAP between 2009 and 2011, accounting for more than a third of total enrollment.

Coauthors Ken Jacobs, Ian Perry, and Jenifer MacGillvary wrote that increasing wages and expanding employer-provided benefits, such as health insurance, could cut Medicare costs and free up money for other programs. Similarly, raising wages could help direct funding for Temporary Assistance for Needy Families (also known as welfare) away from direct cash payments that supplement essential needs toward child care, job training, and other services.

**The minimum wage should have reached $21.72 per hour in 2012,** if it kept up with increases in worker productivity, according to a March 2012 study by the Center for Economic and Policy Research. While advancements in technology have increased the amount of goods and services that can be produced in a set amount of time, wages have remained relatively flat, the study points out. Even if the minimum wage kept up with inflation since it peaked in real value in the late 1960s, low-wage workers should be earning a minimum of $10.52 an hour, according to the study…A Goliath Economic Challenge.

## The National Media Effect

The National Media in the U.S. is controlled by five Major Corporations who combined control 90% of everything we read, see, and hear. THIS MEDIUM SERVES AS THE NUMBER ONE SOURCE USED BY CORPORATE AMERICA AND THE GOVERNMENT TO CONTROL ALL CITIZENS' COGNITIVE MAP – OUR THOUGHTS AND VIEWS. Traditional for-profit media, including our daily newspapers, radio and TV news, filter out all kinds of information they don't want us to get our hands on. This filtering process includes many kinds of stories, including reports that would offend advertisers but, if carried, would alert the public to things such as improper Corporate and Political behavior. Corporate-owned media also slant the content of stories so that some stories paint a negative picture of organized labor, protest groups or racial groups. They also manipulate the way certain racial articles are presented to the general publicand often times create biased commentaries that promote and incite *xenophobic xtti*tudes towards the *disenfranchised*.

On the other hand, what corporate media does allow to freely pass-through the filter, are all kinds of stories that tout capitalism as being good for everyone. They endorse free-market economic practices, even though such policies tend to make the "*poor poorer and the rich richer.*"

According to an article published in*Mic.com* by Eviya Iranovska on March 26, 2012, ABC News Senior White House correspondent Jake Tapper recently suggested that the Obama administration has been aggressively trying to stop qualitative journalism in the U.S. by using the Espionage Act to take whistleblowers to court.

One may agree with this thesis, especially being aware of changes that occurred during the last three decades. When Ben Bagdikian, a former **editor** of the *Washington Post*, published the first edition of the book *The Media Monopoly* in 1983, he estimated that ownership of most of the major media was consolidated in **fifty national and multinational conglomerates**. When he published *The New Media Monopoly* two decades later, Bagdikian concluded that the number had dwindled to **just five.** The U.S. media landscape is dominated by massive corporations that, through a history of mergers and acquisitions, have concentrated their control over what we see, hear and read.

1. **General Electric** (GE) is chief among these, with 2009 revenues standing at $157 billion. GE media-related holdings include a minority share in television networks NBC and Telemundo, Universal Pictures, Focus Features, and twenty-six television stations in the U.S. including cable networks MSNBC, Bravo and the Sci-Fi Channel. Apart from the consumer appliances market, it is also characterized by huge involvement in banking, insurance, and defense industries.

2. **The Walt Disney Corporation**, another one of these six major players, hadthe second biggest income at $36.1 billion in 2009.

3. **News Corporation** follows with $30.4 billion revenue, gained from television and cable networks such as Fox and Fox Business Channel, and print publications including the *Wall Street Journal,* the *New York Post,* and *TV Guide.*

4. The largest media conglomerate in the world is **Time Warner.** Although according to revenues, it takes the fourth place with $25.8 billion in 2009.

5. **Viacom** is the fifth point on this list, with 2009 revenues of $13.6 billion. About nine years ago, this company bought CBS.

**Media also has business interests in other sectors**. CBS and NBC have holdings in the nuclear power industry and technology for electric power generation through nuclear plants. Its 2009 revenues were $13 billion. Viacom own the CBS Television Network, the huge publishing company Simon & Schuster, and CBS Radio. CBS is also the leading supplier of videos to Google....A Global Goliath.

In 1996, under the Clinton administration, the Telecommunications Act was passed. It had more impact on the media landscape than anything that has come before or since. It effectively ended meaningful controls on how much media any one organization could own, more specifically inany one area. Before this law was passed, Murdoch, for example, could not possibly have owned a TV station and a newspaper in the same city.

- As we can see, this structural problem is created by the U.S. government acting hand in hand with private corporations.

## The Good Society

When Sociologist Robert Bellah and his coauthors first published their gut-checking book; (*Creating the Good Society)* in 1991, it became a wake-up call and rallying cry for America.

- The book challenges **Americans** to **look in the mirror** while they are currently pursuing the **American Dream of Individualism** with no regard forour current ills of society.

- They set out to prove that America's social problems confronting us today are largely due to the **failures of our institution and systems** that were originally designed to protect us, yet have now enslaved **us.** We, individually, have been conditioned to believe that we are living the American Dream – pursuing our private satisfactions independently of others.

Today, individualism has all but disappeared in the sense that it existed during the conception of America. Individualism today offers no validation of self-worth or recognition of achievement. Instead, it celebrates selfishness and fear of change. Most Americans have become conformists. Completely absorbed in the pursuit of short-term happiness and gratification we are willing to endure corruption, degradation, and disenfranchisement at the hands of the corporations we helped raise to power. Now, the economic influence of these corporations molds and shapes the culture and morals of its citizens. Our lack of common purpose and concern for the common good, works against the true meaning of democracy. We are so busy chasing that darn "**Golden Rabbit**", we turn a blind eye to the socioeconomic systems that continue to DIVIDE and ENSLAVE us.

- Despite the enactment of various civil and equal rights laws specifically devised to eradicate inequality, most minorities in America today remain disproportionately unprotected from social injustices and inequalities and are made to feel invisible

Most white Americans are born with middle class economic advantages that automatically increase their opportunities to succeed and lead productive lives. While most minorities are born with far less means that definitely lessens their probabilities of success.

America was built on socioeconomic ideals of individualism, that self-reliant sense of empowerment in the face of peril and freedom to reach for the stars.

This bold New Frontier, the land of opportunity, offered unlimited promise for immigrants who came from around the world. Many came with an optimistic entrepreneurial spirit of hope and prosperity beyond imagination which led them to endeavor to develop a new life. New communities were built, beginning with the Virginia Company of London, founded and developed Jamestown in 1607 as the first permanent New-World English Settlement. This new world became a nation of nations, including individuals from all over the world with an array of varied cultural and economic backgrounds. America was the land of the big dreamer where each man could claim fortune in accordance to his efforts and keep what he produced.

## The Great Transformation

After the Second World War, individualism struggled as a result of the Great Depression that occurred from 1933 to 1939. This depression immediately followed the war and changed the socioeconomic landscape of the U.S. entirely. Millions became instantly unemployed, impoverished, and destitute overnight. Servicemen returning home from war were even worse off than the current citizenry. As a result, President Roosevelt and Congress implemented a series of new social entitlement and work programs known as The New Deal. This innovative social initiative, created millions of jobs, Federal financial aid and food assistance that began to take effect during the late 1930's through early 1940's to help stabilize the economy. As the economy began to grow and prosper exponentially, Americans began to view individualism differently. 1946 ushered in the Baby - Boomer generation. This generation became intoxicated by the need to be seen, heard, and admired, giving birth to the Age of Consumerism. Technological advances in consumer electronics and mass media created a perfect storm of generating and satisfying consumer demand.

Today, individualism is consumed by capitalistic ambitions. *Me-Me-Me* has created a misguided existence of delusion for most Americans.

## Economic Inequality

In accordance with a very provocative and compelling article posted by *Nation of Change* on January 11, 2016, by Paul Buchheit, *"The Real Terrorists: The .01%"*

Approximately 16,000 individuals, the Untouchables, 1% who control 80% of the total U.S. wealth, continue to create an inequality nightmare for the 50% of Americans who are in or near poverty. They are also now impacting those who previously deemed themselves safely protected, those in the second highest wealth quartile, i.e. upper middle income brackets. With the continuous decline of the U.S. middle class, the tax burden is exponentially shifting more and more to this second upper income bracket.

The combined net worth of the 16,000 richest Americans is approximately the same as the total wealth of 256,000,000 people which represents 80% of the total U.S. population and includes all citizens with a net worth up to a maximum of $277,000.

The 1% own about as much as 75% of the entire world's wealth. The world's poorest 75% own roughly four percent of the total global wealth, approximately the same percentage of wealth owned by the top 1% in the United States.

The top 1% starts with the billionaires, the Forbes 400 and 136 more, for a total of 536 individuals with a total net worth of $2.6 trillion at the end of 2015. It continues with more ultra-high net worth individuals (UHNWIs). These loftily-named people, over 16,000 of them, are worth hundreds of millions of dollars apiece, bringing the total 1% wealth to about $6.2 trillion, based on 2013-14 data.

U.S. wealth has grown by about thirty percent in three years, and the Forbes 400 has grown by thirty-eight percent. Thus, the total wealth of the 1% has grown to over $9 trillion. In contrast, the bottom 75% of America owned about $6.2 trillion in 2013.

The majority of the 1%'s wealth has and is being generated honestly. However, instead of paying their fair share of taxes, they've all formed somewhat of an income defense industry to shelter their riches through employing some of the brightest and most sophisticated Lawyers, Estate Planners, Lobbyists, and Anti-Tax Lobbyists, who, exploit and defend a vast array of tax avoidance strategies that are financially beyond the reach of the general public.

## Economic Terrorism

As the 1% go about their self-serving tax avoidance business, 2.5 million children experience homelessness every year. The corporations of the 1% hoard hundreds of billions overseas while nearly two-thirds of American families don't have enough money to replace a broken furnace.

Most are so arrogant and delusional about their inherited status and are thus classified as follows:

*   "They were born on third base, but are delusional in thinking they hit a triple."(Coach Barry Switzer).

This is real terror, facing life without shelter and warmth and sustenance, without a semblance of security for even one day in the future. It is terror caused in good part by the 16,000 people who don't feel it's necessary to pay for the benefits heaped upon them by a perversely unequal society.

*   These unrelenting and insensitive social terrorist believe they are above the law and since many of them are private members of the invisible government  syndication, simply consider themselves untouchable.

What most of them fail to realize is the fact that – *"There's a great equalizer over the entire universe who always balances the scale no matter how big you think you are."*

## Social Effects of Wealth Disparity

The twentieth century political philosopher John Rawls argued that extreme economic inequality undermines the real possibility of equal democratic citizenship. The reason for this is that the drastic gap between the very rich and the rest of us creates two types of citizens, with the rich having much greater control over the political process because of their wealth.

Even Alan Greenspan, the former Federal Reserve Chairman has expressed concern about the disparity between the wealthy and the middle-class. Greenspan worried that the large disparity between the rich and everyone else would undermine the faith in capitalism held by the average system.

Capitalism cannot be sustained over time in a democracy if people begin to doubt that the system benefits them as well as the wealthy. Such a view throws the system into crisis. In many ways, this is the current public perception of the government bailouts. We all feel tight. Some of us are out of work. But whom is the government helping? Banks and corporations, eventhough 80% of the American public voted against the financial bailouts in 2009-2010. However, our government proceeded to give out a combined $1.4 trillion dollars to banks and corporations relying on unverifiable Too-Big-To-Fail justifications. Now this is not totally fair, as all benefit from a healthy financial system. But, as we look at the huge disparity between the wealthy and the rest of us, we are justified in being skeptical as to whether any of these efforts really trickle down. The minimum wage rate of $7.25 per hour today, is the same as in 1968 (adjusted for inflation). How are people supposed to get ahead when they're struggling to survive?

Today, the 160 million U.S.citizens living in or near poverty, have been inequitably debased.

- Ultimately, the obstacle that keeps us from adequately addressing our most pressing economic and social problems is our inability to see others as ourselves. Theorists of deliberative democracy have called this reciprocity, the ability to put ourselves in the position of others. John Rawls referred to this as our capacity to treat others as free and equal citizens. From a Christian perspective, we must ask ourselves whether we view all human beings as valuable Children of God?

# Corruption

The U.S. economic and political inseparability has resulted in formulating a Plutocratic Society governed by the rich which has created two distinct sub-societies: Socialism for the Rich and Capitalism (Trickle-down Economics) for the Poor. This current socioeconomic system is beyond race, class, and quotas.

Until major corporate donors and lobbyists are taken out of the political process, we will never have an unbiased governing republic capable of regulating the corrupt Western economic system that enslaves the people.

Jacob (Mormon Prophet) takes a different approach to answering this question. What we really need is not a different way of thinking about wealth, but we need to re-evaluate how we view our fellow human beings.

Jacob says that we should think of [our] brethren like unto [ourselves]. If we do, then it will follow that we will be familiar with all and be free with [our] substance, that they may be rich like unto [us] (Jacob 2:17).

"There is no future for mankind unless tolerance and understanding between cultures and nations become the rule instead of the exception" (UN Secretary General Kurt Waldheim 2012).

- *We must all learn to reconcile our differences and develop a change of heart. This is the beginning of reconciliation.*

# Chapter 9

# Imminent Danger

*An uneducated Society shall never prosper.*

## U.S. Education System Today

**THE U.S. SPENDS SIGNIFICANTLY MORE ON EDUCATION** than any other countries in the Organization for Economic Cooperation and Development (OECD), which is comprised of the World's Top 34 largest economies. In 2010, the U.S. spent 39 % more per full-time student for elementary and secondary education than the average for other OECD Countries. Yet, it only ranked as the fourteenth most educated society in the world.

### *Every Student Succeeds Act (ESSA)*

As reported in *The U.S. News and World Report – "The Conversation"* on *December 14, 2015*, "the most significant National Education Reform Law – Every Student Succeeds Act (ESSA) was passed by the House and Senate and signed into law by President Barack Obama on December 10, 2015," and becomes effective in the 2017 – 18 school year.

This new law replaces the controversial **No Child Left Behind (NCLB)**, which was implemented in 2001. Over the last fourteen years, NCLB has faced many challenges for reform. While many changes had been proposed, the House and Senate failed to agree on such changes.

Will the Every Student Succeeds Act live up to its name and assure equal educational opportunity for every one of America's fifty million public school children?

The main difference between NCLB and ESSA is that ESSA hands the educational accountability ball down from the federal government to the states.

**ESSA** is better, because it rightly takes aim at test and assessment strategies, and creates some valuable programs. But ESSA, like NCLB, **emphasizes K-12 accountability over root causes of educational inequality**. And the new law flies against history's lesson that federal oversight is a good thing for vulnerable children.

## What Makes ESSABetter?

Organizations with widely divergent views on education agree that the ESSA should replace NCLB.

- It provides more flexibility on testing. It also ends *Adequate Yearly Progress* – a measure that required schools to show test score gains. Schools that failed to meet goals were penalized.

- It provides preschool development grants for low-income children and an arts education fund.

- The new law drops the term core academic subjects and uses instead a well-rounded education, meaning that subjects like social studies and arts are less likely to be what one study called collateral.

- The ESSA also stops the practice of putting multiple student subgroups (students with disabilities and low-income students, for example) into super subgroups – a practice that can mask inequities.

But these changes are more about what's bad in our current policies than what's good in the new bill.

## Testing versus Anti-Poverty

In 2013, for the first time, low-income children (defined as living in households where the income is no more than 185 % of the poverty threshold) became the majority in U.S. public schools, prompting the Southern Education Foundation to warn that unless we provide more for these students, the trends of the last decade will be prologue for a nation not at risk, but a nation in decline.

What is the new law's solution to this?

Testing mandates in the ESSA continue the retreat from the anti-poverty focus of the 1965 Elementary and Secondary Education Act. In signing that act, President Lyndon Johnson (LBJ) identified poverty as the greatest barrier to educational opportunity, and under Title I provided $1 billion for schools with large numbers of poor children.

- That means the ESSA will likely do little to disrupt the NCLB pattern of punishing vulnerablechildren and the low performance of the schools they attend. This will not fix achievement gaps.

Though Title I is central to the ESSA; LBJ's understanding that educational achievement depends on civil and economic rights is largely absent.

Expanding Opportunity through Quality Charter Schools section of ESSA is the proposed alternative to the current nationwide school closing initiative for underperforming/low enrollment/Title I Schools. Yet Charters have a decidedly mixed record, particularly with English language learners and children with disabilities.

- Basically, the ESSA's support for Charter Schools reflects the Federal Government's continued gravitation towards total autonomy from its National obligation to educate all of her children.

"History has taught us that each and every time the Federal Government has relinquished its Public obligations to protect and provide for all the Citizens of this Nation over to State Governments and third parties, it has always produced some watered down-manipulated version of the original Intent of the Law."

As long as attention remains on testable accountability in K-12 schools rather than on poverty, inequality and early education, every student succeeds act, like no child left behind, will continue to be an unfulfilled promise.

## The Numbers Don't Lie

The 2014 National High School Graduation Rate was **82%.** This was a historic U.S. high. The breakdown of graduation rates for each ethnic group in 2014 were: Asian Pacific 93%, White 85%, Black 68%, Hispanic 76%, Native American/Alaskan Natives 68%. Of the nearly 3.0 million youth age 16 to 24 who graduated from high school between January and October 2013, about 2.0 million (**65.9%**) were enrolled in college in October. **The college enrollment rate of recent**

**high school graduates in October2013,** was little different from the rate in October 2012 (**66.2%**). For 2013graduates, the college enrollment rate was **68.4%**for young women and **63.5%**for young men. The college enrollment rate of Asians, at79.1%, was higher than the rates for recent White (**67.1%**), Black (**59.3%**), and Hispanic (**59.**9 %) graduates. More alarming is the fact that **52.1% of all eligible High School students never attend College;**(18% national High School dropout rate plus 34.1% of the High Schoolgraduates who don't attend College).

- According to a recent Federal Reserve Report released on May 5, 2014, the average College Graduate earns $830,000 more than a High School Graduate over their productive lives and contributes $278,000 more to their respective local Economies than High School Graduates nationwide.

*The U.S. has been the historical dominant player in College Educated Citizens worldwide for the last 90 years but today only rank* fourteenth worldwide. College Institutions today are experiencing record increases in enrollments. However, the average dropout rates hover around 30%. Of the remaining 70% that do graduate, only 54% graduate from a four-year school.

- College education today presents a challenging dilemma for most high school students. Most understand quite well the increased lifetime income realities, yet remain precautious about the lifetime financial traps of student loans.

## College Education Parable:
*"College Education today is comparable to purchasing a new house with a price tag that scares you because you fear another market financial collapse and being stuck upside-down in a bad mortgage for thirty years."*

## All Youth Enrolled in High School or College
In October 2013, **56.6%**of the nation's 16 to 24year-olds, or **22.0 million young people**, were enrolled in high school (**9.5 million**) or in college (**12.5 million**). The labor force participation rate was **37.2%** and the unemployment rate, **11.7%** for youth enrolled in school in October 2013. For both high school and college students, **jobless rates for Blacks and Hispanics were 50% higher than for Whites**.

## *All Youth not enrolled in School*

In October 2013, **16.8 million** people age 16 to 24 were not enrolled in school. The labor force participation rate of youth not enrolled in school was **77.7 %** in October 2013. The unemployment rate of **16.1%** for youth age 16 to 24 not enrolled in school in October 2013, was essentially unchanged from October 2012. **Among non-enrolled youth who did not have a high school diploma**, unemployment rates in October 2013, were **26.4%** for young men and **32.9%** for young women.

**In 2013,** the College Graduate education pool is estimated to be **1,744,000.** Women will comprise 57% of the total, surpassing men. It will also be the most **diverse graduating class in U.S. History with Hispanics showing the most significant gains at 25%** and STEM (Science/Technology/Engineering/Math) majors representing10% of total graduates). Today, more high growth opportunities exist in STEM fields, however, the talent pool is consistently deficient. Although many national and local educational efforts have been geared toward increasing STEM participation at earlier ages, participation has remained flat for the last five years. The biggest labor challenge in the U.S. today is shortage of qualified college graduates in general and more specifically STEM graduates. This dilemma has forced many major corporations to outsource, insource, or contract for many highly specialized occupations. While this is considered a temporary solution, it remains a growing trend and results in increased unemployment for new non-STEM College Graduates and other displaced prospective employees as well.

• A closer look at the overall numbers shows that if you have 3,650,000 Baby Boomers retiring annually and only 1,744,000 potentially qualified College Graduates to fill vacant or newly created jobs, the U.S. would experience job losses totaling1,906,000 per year. If we endeavor to look even closer at the additional 1,000,000 high school grads that never attend college, of which 936,000 enter the job market directly into low paying/skill minimum wage jobs and the additional 629,000 high school dropouts who normally wander in the desert for a few years, representing a delayed employment entry, we find 1,906,000 remaining Baby boomer job vacancies of which, only 936,000 could reasonably be absorbed thus leaving a huge labor Gap of approximately 920,000 vacated jobs. This does not include new job creations or job eliminations every year for the next 18 years or worse.

**U.S. Population Shift (Minority – Majority):**

**There are 49.5 million total U.S. Public School Children enrolled in grades K through 12** and their racial profile is changing rapidly: White – 52%, Black – 16%, Hispanic – 24%, Asian – 5%, Native American Indian – 1%, and Biracial – 3%. The Hispanic school age population is growing faster than any other ethnic group. From 2001 to 2011; Hispanic public school enrollments increased from 17% to 24%, and is projected to out pace all other ethnicities going forward. Currently, minority Public School total enrollments represent 48% with Hispanics representing half of that percentage. This is primarily due to the explosive projected future Hispanic growth, which is expected to increase 33% from 2012 – 2022. The **total School Age population in the U.S. is projected to go from a Majority-Minority to a historic Minority-Majority population by 2018.**

# Discipline: School Children

A recent Assessment performed by the Center for the Study of Race and Equity in Education at the University of Pennsylvania Graduate School of Education in August 2015, concluded that African American school children are more likely to be suspended or expelled at three times the rate of Whites nationwide and five times more likely in the South. Most Social Scientist attribute this massive social deficiency to the fact that the vast majority of these children are raised without fathers in the home which makes them more susceptible to experience emotional and behavioral problems,more likely to be expelled from school or dropout of school, and to engage in crime. In addition, income, family instability, economics, and population segregation are undeniably contributing realities that shape the course of their journey.

Unequal punishment of Black students happens in places that are dissimilar from each other—in rich and poor districts as well as ones that are predominantly Black or majority White. The root cause of these disparities can be found in Nationwide Zero-Tolerance School Policies and its unequitable enforcement by School Administrators. The data speaks not only to a real history and legacy of discrimination that still lingers in the South, along with modern perceptual biases that lead educators to see African American students more negatively than Whites for the same behaviors. What's different is the adult reaction to the behavior. Unequal punishment of Black and White students is a factor in the school-to-prison pipeline and deprives Black children of a quality education. Correcting this is a key to closing the stubborn Achievement Gap.

- The U.S. Government starts planning Prison Facility Development based on National third grade disciplinary statistics which goes to follow the Theory of School-to-Prison Pipeline that starts with minority school aged children being disciplined at three to five times the rate of white children, thus convincingly fueling the current 2.2 million U.S. prison population, which is comprised of 80% minorities.

Solutions are in reach, starting with giving rich and poor schools equal resources and teaching Educator's about racial sensitivity. There's a lack of professional development with respect to behavior and classroom management at schools of education and other sites in which teachers and school leaders are credentialed and certified.

- In October2015, a fourteen-year-old Muslim child Ahmed Mohamed, in Dallas, Texas, was suspended from school for three days because his teacher mistook his home made clock for a bomb displaying her apparent xenophobic attitude to the world. Making matters worse, top school officials supported her actions. Only after a public outcry on social media, where even President Obama waged his disbelief, did the school recant their overreaction even though they refused to overturn his three day suspension. In lieu of serving the suspension, his parents transferred him to another school.

As a result of this nationally publicized incident and countless others, along with ongoing disproportionate discipline reports between the races of school children nationwide, many big city school districts have begun to implement new discipline program policies to specifically address these rapidly developing challenges. School Districts in New York, Los Angeles, and Denver have taken a more proactive approach of Counseling versus Suspensions and providing better training for School Officials to deal with Conflict Resolution. Other States such as Oregon, limit suspension and expulsion of all students until after fifth grade. Denver's Whole Child Support System leads the way in that it experienced a year-to-year reduction from 11,500 out-of-school suspensions in 2013 to 5,400 in 2014 (53% reduction) and 167 Expulsions in 2013 to 55 in 2014 (67% reduction).

# Diversity Gap:

## *Student Population*

In 2012, only 23% of Black and Latino students attended  majority White schools. This is exactly the same percentage as in 1968.This statistic also confirms similar White segregation patterns within the communities that house these majority White schools. The remaining 77% of Black and Latino school aged kids attend predominately Minority-Majority schools.

According to new studies by the Civil Rights Project, Guy Orfield undeniably suggests that increased levels of segregation in U.S. public schools are so substantial that the authors conclude, "**The U.S. success as a multiracial society is at risk**."

## *U.S. Enrollment Growing Rapidly More Diverse*

*   In 1970, nearly four out of every five students across the nation were White. By 2009, just over 50% were White.

*   **Latino** enrollment has soared from **one-twentieth** of U.S. students in 1970 to nearly **one-fourth** (22.8%).Latino students have become the dominant minority group in the Western half of the country.

*   **White** students account for just **52% of U.S. first graders**, forecasting future change.

## *Double School Segregation by Race and Poverty*

*   The typical **Black** or **Latino** today attends school with almost double the share of low-income students in their schools than the typical **White** or **Asian** student.

- In the early **1990s**, the average Latino and Black student attended a school where roughly **one-third** of students were low income (as measured by free and reduced price lunch eligibility), but now attend schools where low income students account for nearly **two-thirds** of their classmates.

## *Racial Segregation Deepens for Black and Latino Students*

- In spite of the dramatic suburbanization of non-White families, 80% of Latino students and 74% of Black students attend majority non-White schools, and 43% of Latinos and 38% of Blacks attend intensely segregated schools across the nation, those with only 0-10%White students. On **average, 77% of all Black and Hispanic school aged kids attend Minority-Majority Schools Nationwide.**

- 15% of Black students and 14% of Latino students attend apartheid schools across the nation, where Whites make up 0 to1% of the enrollment.

- Latino students in nearly every region have experienced steadily rising levels of concentration in intensely segregated minority settings. In the West, the share of Latino students in such settings has increased fourfold, from 12% in 1968 to 43% in 2009.

- Eight of the twenty states reporting the highest numbers of students attending schools under apartheid conditions are located in the South or in US states that border Mexico. This is a significant retrenchment on civil rights progress. The number of Apartheid schools nationwide has mushroomed from 2,768 in 1988, the peak of public school integration, to 6,727 in 2011.

- The nation's largest metropolitan areas report severe school racial concentration. Half of the Black students in the Chicago metro area and one third of Black students in New York attend Apartheid Schools.

- Latino students experience high levels of extreme segregation in the Los Angeles metro area, where roughly 30% attend a school in which Whites make up 1% or less of the enrollment.

**White students are isolated with other White students. Black and Latino students have little contact with White students.**

- Though Whites make up just over 50% of the nation's enrollment, the typical White student attends a school where 75% of their peers are white.

- White students account for about 64% of the total enrollment in the Northeast, but the typical Black student attends a school with only 25% whites.

- Exposure to White students for the average Latino student has decreased dramatically over theyears for every Western State, particularly in California, where the average Latino student had 54.5% White peers in 1970 but only 16.5% in 2009.

- *High-poverty, segregated black and Latino schools account for the majority of roughly 1,400 high schools nationwide labeled "**dropout factories**" meaning fewer than **60 percent** of the students graduate.*

An excerpt from a Nicole Hannah-Jones article, Segregation Now – 2014 Study conducted by Rucker Johnson, a public-policy professor at the University of California at Berkeley, published by the National Bureau of Economic Research.

Notably, Johnson found that Black progress did not come at the expense of White Americans. White students in integrated schools did just as well academically as those in segregated schools. Other studies have found that attending integrated schools made White students more likely to later live in integrated neighborhoods and send their own children to racially diverse schools. Additionally, *low-income students placed in middle-income schools show marked academic progress.*

Most minority kids that are deemed high poverty attend predominately segregated elementary schools and by the time they start eighth grade, Black students are already three years behind their White counterparts in math and reading. In most of these re-segregating districts, school administrators proclaim they are going to focus on raising test scores at "every" school while being delusional about the reality of not being properly equipped to succeed.

## Teacher Population

According to the Center for American Progress study in 2015, while almost 50% of U.S. public school children are minorities, only 20% of U.S. teachers are non-White. There were about 3.3 million teachers in American public elementary and secondary schools in 2012, according to a study by the National Center for Education Statistics - 82% were White, 8% Hispanic, 7% Black and about 2% Asian. This diversity gap is real and continues to plague and hamper minority student performance accordingly. It becomes easier for students to believe in the teacher and quality of instruction when they can look and see someone who looks just like them that they can relate to.

• More than minority students would benefit from a more diverse teacher corps because it's important for our social fabric, for our sense as a nation, for students to engage with people who think, talk and act differently than them who are also just as effective at raising student achievement in the classroom.

A recent extensive report by the Albert Shanker Institute confirms that while the percentage of minority teachers has risen in the U.S., the number of Black teachers has declined between 2002 and 2012 in nine cities (Boston, Chicago, Cleveland, Los Angeles, New Orleans, Philadelphia, San Francisco and Washington D.C.).

"Diversity is a key component to equality and opportunity," says Randi Weingarten, president of the American Federation of Teachers. "Where there's a diverse teaching workforce, all kids thrive. That's why we note with alarm the sharp decline in the population of Black teachers in our cities."

There are several factors which may be behind this decline. The first is low pay for teachers. According to a study by Young Invincibles, an advocacy group, the average starting salary for a teacher is $34,575, about $6,000 less than the average starting salary of twenty-eight other professions.

"The second is the recurring emphasis that education policy tends to place on test scores in that this rigidity," argues Nikita Lamour, a Haitian-American and tenured educator, "disincentivises Black and Hispanic educators from participating in the system. They are not being encouraged to teach their fellow man, but to the test, instead."

The Shanker Institute's study found that over a ten-year period, from 2002 to 2012 (a period marked by an explosion in the development of Charter schools and an accompanying dialogue about education reform), the population of Black teachers declined by as much as 62% in the cities studied. Although in the case of New Orleans, many Black teachers were fired.

"Minority teachers quit because of working conditions in their schools," Richard Ingersoll, an expert who teaches at the University of Pennsylvania, also told the Washington Post. "In surveys, those teachers cite lack of autonomy and input into school decisions [in large urban schools]."

There is also evidence that suggests Black and Hispanic teachers are crucial to an effective school system, especially to minority-majority districts. Not only do they serve as a role model to young kids who may not be acquainted with many college-educated adults, they also have what the study terms heritage knowledge, or an ingrained understanding of the culture in which they operate because they are from it. This so-called heritage knowledge can lessen the barrier of educational accessibility for minority students, because they are being taught by adults who are from their own backgrounds.

## Funding Gap:

The Center for American Progress, an independent bipartisan educational institute, released a report in August 2015 that the Elementary and Secondary Education Act includes a loophole that keeps financial resources from the kids who can least afford it, the more than 4.5 million low-income (Title 1) students at 12,000 public schools nationwide.

- The so-called Comparative Loophole linked to Title I Federal funding, according to the report, is responsible for a $1,200 per student funding gap between wealthy districts and struggling ones.

If that loophole was closed, poor districts would have access to $8.5 billion more per year in government funds.

- At issue is a Title I requirement that rich and poor districts provide comparable educational services in order to receive federal money. But the law, as written, allows districts to qualify as comparable using either average teacher salaries or student-to-teacher ratios.

National Bureau of Economic Research Study shows that given sufficient resources, students in poor communities are more likely to stay in school, earn better grades, and graduate. That study also declares the U.S. is one of only three OECD countries that allocate less money to educate students from poor backgrounds than others.

## *Our inequitable school funding system is a national disgrace.*

According to a *Washington Post* article, some argue that if you remove the test scores of students in poverty from America's performance, our test scores are among the best in the world. Then, they say, you are comparing apples with apples since we have a much higher poverty rate than most other countries.

## *National Report Card*

The U.S. Public School System realized an 82% National High School graduation rate for the 2013-14 school year; this national all-time record actually only represents a 1% increase from the 2012-13 rate of 81%.

Now, many experts are raising concerns about the True Value of a High School Diploma and questioning whether the requirements are too lax and easy. Many of their concerns stem mainly from the fact that many states differ on high school graduation requirements from number of credits to testing; and there currently exists no National Benchmark Qualification. As a result, many disturbing trends are surfacing to include the fact that high percentages of today's graduates are Lacking College Ready and Career Ready Skills Nationwide.

- The most recent evaluation of twelfth graders on National Tests for Reading and Math found that fewer than 40% were College Ready. This continues to plague College aspirations, requiring students to first enroll in College Remediation Classes which too often result in extended college matriculation and increased dropout rates. This is especially true at two-year community colleges, where fewer than 33% who enroll complete a degree within three years. The numbers are even worse for Blacks and Hispanics.

Many business industry leaders have similar concerns in their assessments of recent high school graduate applicants, noting that most lack basic collaboration and effective communication skills not being taught at the high school level.

• The majority of the applicants are not passing many of the simplest cognitive tests required for most entry level jobs.

This alarming dilemma has prompted many industry leaders to conclude that, the current U.S. education system is preparing graduates for a work environment that doesn't exist today. Something has to change and that has to be our education system.

• According to a recent *AJC* Education Report, January 7, 2016 – 44% of new Georgia teachers leave the profession within five years mainly due to their frustration with being mandated to focus more on Test Preparation thanTeaching.

## *There's a Big Difference between:*
*Test preparation and testing– Giving lessons and Taking Tests; Education in the U.S. today*

*Teaching and learning– Taught with Understanding; Where U.S. Education needs to be.*

• TESTING versus TEACHING-Teachers truly want to make a difference in students' lives which goes far beyond just preparing them to pass tests.

• "Many Students give correct answers on tests, but fail to put those lessons into practice – Undigested Knowledge" (Lancelot Oliphant).

## *Case in Point:*
One of my greatest educational learning experiences occurred while matriculating as an Undergraduate Management Science major at Tuskegee University. It occurred in my junior year while actively enrolled in an Operations Management course. This course proved to

be both challenging and rewarding to the extent that I became one of the class leaders and actually tutored some of my fellow classmates who were struggling in the course.

**As we neared the end of the course**, I carried a B+ average going into the final exam which was to account for 40% of our final grade. Two weeks prior to taking the Final Exam, an uncontrollable circumstance occurred. I was living off campus in a rented house with a roommate. We were both informed by our landlord that they had a relative moving in town from Kentucky and needed a place to stay and since they owned the house we were renting as well as the house next door, they had already informed their relative they would have a choice between the two houses which happened to be very similar in style and space but different in color. Bear in mind that in this small country town, it was customary that many of the landlords refused to sign formal leases with the college student population and thus most rented on a verbal month to month basis, as did we.

**The relatives arrived**, toured both houses, and surprisingly chose our house over our neighbors. We had two days to move. Although we filed legal action and eventually prevailed, we still were required to move most of our possessions and furnishings into storage and physically move in with friends which totally disrupted all sense of normalcy. As a result, I was unable to commit the quality study time required to prepare for all of my finals. Although I did well, obtaining a B or better on all except Operations Management. I ended up with a 79. Since the final accounted for 40%, it effectively lowered my final grade to a C (80). Of course, I was very distraught and disappointed.

**Afterwards**, I requested a meeting with my professor, Dr. Sara. He was my primary professor for most of my core required management classes and one of my biggest supporters. Upon meeting with him and venting my frustrations, he exhibited great compassion in understanding my dilemma. Once I finished explaining, he asked me one question: "What would you have me to do?" In response, I thanked him for listening and understanding. He then asked another question, "In spite of your final grade, do you think you mastered the material?" My response was absolutely. He agreed, and further reminded me that understanding how to apply the knowledge far outweighed the grade for the course. **In that moment, I clearly understood the value of learning versus merely studying for a grade.**

According to a 2013 National Assessment of Education Program (NAEP) – 66% of U.S. fourth graders are below grade level in reading (80% of Low Income Students). Also, the U.S. ranked just twenty-seventh out of thirty-four OECD Countries for eighth grade math achievement.

- Overall, the majority of all U.S. children cannot read or compute at grade level and with nearly 75% of Blacks and Latino's falling short, it poses a great national economic and security threat for America.

We currently have 49 million citizens living in poverty of which 15.5 million are children; 70% are children of color, mainly comprised of Blacks (37%) and Hispanics (32%). The remaining 30% is comprised of Whites (12%) and all other ethnicities collectively. This challenge is a national socioeconomic travesty. By 2018, the U.S. school age population will go from a Majority-Majority to a Majority-Minority school-aged population for the first time in our nations' history whereby this new majority will be comprised of predominately minority poverty students.

- Every year, we allow millions of children to remain in poverty. It costs our nation in excess of $500 billion in lost productivity, extra healthcare costs, and crime costs respectively.

## Schools with High Poverty Rates:

A recent *New York Times* article states that just over half of all students attending public schools in the United States are now eligible for free or reduced-price lunches, according to a new analysis of federal data. In a report released in September 2015 by Southern Education Foundation, researchers found that 51% of children in public schools qualified for the federal lunch program in 2013, which means that most of them come from low-income families. By comparison, 38% of public school students were eligible for free or reduced-price lunches in 2000. In direct contrast, in 2015, there currently exists a total of 98,817 U.S. public operating schools of which 56,000 (56.7%) are Title 1 Schools, schools in which a minimum of 40% of the total student body are eligible for reduced or free lunch which also qualifies these schools to be eligible for additional government educational funding in order to close the apparent Achievement Gap experienced by low income students.

Poverty rates in this country are disturbingly high, among the highest in the developed world. Children cannot learn when they are afraid to walk to school, when they are hungry all day, when they are housed in ugly deteriorating school buildings, when *they never encounter a gifted teacher.* While there are extraordinary exceptions, the weakest teachers tend to be assigned to the highest poverty schools. Poverty is a major factor impeding school achievement in this country.

- Our country was built on the idea that everyone gets an equal shot. Our education system is the foundation of that equal shot and right now it's cracking for students who start with less.

As the percentage of White students in our educational system shrinks and the percentage of students of color grow, the U.S. will be left with an education system that doesn't serve the majority of its children properly. The gaps in education will prove especially problematic unless we can all see and move beyond *xenophobia* permanently.

## Education Achievement Gap:

The U.S. President's Council on Jobs and Economic Competitiveness has identified strengthening education as a top priority for preparing the American workforce to compete in the global economy. The Council found that 3.3 million jobs go unfilled because the potential workforce does not have matching skills or training, and that by 2020 there will be 1.5 million too few college graduates to meet employers' demands. A better educated workforce will lower unemployment and enable businesses to more efficiently produce the level of goods and services the market demands.

A more diverse workforce brings with it a better understanding of cultures and potential new markets around the world and a greater variety of perspectives, which in turn leads to greater innovation in products and services. Research has shown that businesses with a more diverse workforce have more customers, higher revenues and profits, greater market share, less absenteeism and turnover, and a higher level of commitment to their organization.

In direct contradiction to the U.S.President's Council on Jobs and Economic Competiveness recommendation of strengthening education as a top priority for preparing the American workforce to compete in the Global Economy is the fact that, according to a recent 2015 report by the American Academy of Arts and Sciences, lawmakers *in eleven state spend more on Prisons than Universities* (Michigan, Oregon, Arizona, Vermont, Colorado, Pennsylvania, New Hampshire, Delaware, Rhode Island, Massachusetts, and Connecticut). According to the report, state budgets for Public Universities have been cut about 20 % since 2008 when the recession hit, while funding for Prisons spiked 141%. More than two-thirds of state prison inmates are high school dropouts according to U.S. Secretary of Education Arne Duncan. African-American males between the ages of 20 and 24 without a High School Diploma or GED have a higher chance of being imprisoned than being employed. A 2014 report from the Center on Budget and Policy Priorities (CBPP) shows a direct correlation between increased prison spending and cuts in Education. States with the highest incarceration rates, pull the most money from their Schools which according to a recent CNN Report, drives up tuition at Public Universities. State funding accounts for about 50% of a typical school's budget. The other 50% comes from the Federal Government and tuition and fees.

In Georgia alone, the Educational Achievement Gap (average Georgia educationl level versus level Employers need) is deficient by 250,000 graduates. This means that in order for Georgia to support its economic development and growth, the State must produce 250,000 more graduates by 2020 than it currently is on schedule to produce. The only way possible for this to happen is to devise a Program that effectively addresses the educational needs of minorities with a critical emphasis on blacks and hispanics.

In 2014, Georgia's High School graduation rate was only 71%. The national average was 82%. Only 10% of Georgia'sHigh School students participate in some type of Cooperative Education, Internship, Apprenticeship or Clinical Program. According to a September 2015

*Atlanta Journal Constitution (AJC )* report, by 2020, 60% of all Georgia jobs will require Post-Secondary Education while currently only 38% of Georgia's High School Sophomores get that far. Furthermore, Georgia spends only $9,402 per student on vocational education and ranks 34th nationally. A few local manufacturing corporations have started to take initiative by devising their own technical training programs to ensure future growth. Southwire is leading the way with their Twelve-for-Life Program which is a High School Apprenticeship Program that allows High School Students to obtain on-the-job training, college credits, and job guarantee upon High School graduation. Although this program has been somewhat successful in training and employing 300 plus Georgia High School Graduates to date, demand continues to outpace supply. Many other Manufacturers are following suit throughout Georgia with reasonable success. However, these are mere isolated independent initiatives that yield minimal impact on the massive demand for Job-Ready Talent. Additionally, Georgia recently launched a New Strategic Industry Program which offers Free College Technical Education to students pursuing Truck Driving, Welding, and Computer technology careers.

According to an August 2015 Georgia Budget and Policy Report, Georgia ranks 9th nationally for having the most Adults age 18 to 64 without a High School Diploma or GED. That is 866,000 people, 14% of the working age population and 61 % minority. According to Melissa Johnson, policyanalyst, Georgia's economic well-being is threatened by the high number of adults without a High School Diploma or a General Equivalency Development credential (GED).

Georgia's adult education programs served only about 60,600 adults in 2014. Georgia's leaders recognize that its citizens must be more educated for the state to compete in a national and global economy that demands more high-skilled workers. Evidence of this includes Gov. Nathan Deal's launch of the Complete College Georgia Initiative in August 2011 to significantly increase the number of Georgians with postsecondary school credentials, thoughresults have been minimal to date. As recent as September 2015, the Governor issued a renewed pledge to produce an additional 250,000 graduates by 2025 which at the current pace appears to be more of a pipedream than a reality. Even if the stars aligned perfectly and this goal was met, Georgia would still remain 250,000 graduates short.By 2025, Georgia will need to have produced an additional 250,000 Graduates based on current work-force projections.

The state will need 250,000 additional graduates with a certificate, associate's degree, bachelor's degree or higher to meet its workforce needs by 2020, according to the initiative. Transforming adult learners into college graduates is an important step in Georgia's plan to meet this goal.

## The DACA Dilemma: Structured Racism – Economic Handicap

Additionally, according to a recent AJC report"*Jim Crow now Juan Crow in Georgia*" by Angela D. Meltzer, Georgia is among a handful of States that refuse to allow Students who meet the criteria of the Federal Governments Deferred Action for Childhood Arrivals (DACA) Policy to pay in–state tuition rates at public colleges. Their parents brought them here without legal sanction and they attended and graduated from Georgia Public High Schools where many excelled academically,speak fluent english, and have never been convicted of a felony, but Georgia only sees them as Illegal Immigrants, Aliens.

The Federal Government considers such students Legally Present which prevents their deportation, allows them to work, and provides them a Social Security Number although they cannot apply for U.S. Citizenship. President Obama's recently revised Immigration Executive actions dated November 20, 2014, further clarified and extended these rights and benefits.

At the State level, *Legally Present* is normally sufficient to qualify for In-State Tuition rates, but not in Georgia. In 2013, Department of Homeland security, declared all DACA Students to be Lawfully Present. The Georgia Board of regents however, continues to deny In-State Tuition to DACA Students based on semantical delusions.  In 2008, GA Senate Bill 492 prohibited In-State Tuition to Unauthorized Immigrants Georgia Board of Regents Policy 4.3.4 requires *Lawful Presence* to qualify for In-State tuition rates, so are they saying that Georgia's definition of Lawful Presence is different from Department of Homeland Security definition of Lawfully Present? These are apparently some mean spirited semantics to say the least. Currently in the U.S., a total of 31 out of 50 States have adopted DACA In-State Tuition and Out-of-State Tuition Policies that range from all State Colleges to restricted State Colleges. The other nineteen States; have no DACA in-state tuition, nor out-of-state tuition Policy.

- While more than twenty-two states allow undocumented students to attend public universities or qualify for in-state tuition, *Georgia is the only State in the country* to ban students both from select universities and from in-state tuition. Because undocumented students are ineligible for federal financial aid, these policies effectively exclude undocumented students and usher in a modern era of educational segregation in the South.

DACA Students in Georgia attending Public Colleges are required to pay Out-of-State Tuition which is often three to four times the cost of In-State Tuition. With most being academically inclined from impoverished families, they typically go to school for a semester and sit out working the alternate semester to fund the next. In 2010, The Board of Regents further prohibited DACA Students from attending Georgia's Top 5 University's (UGA, Georgia Tech, GA State, Medical College of GA, and GA College and State University) under any conditions.

## A Sliver of Hope:

According to a *Huffington Post* College Article,"Freedom University: Georgia Professors Offer Course to Undocumented Immigrants" (AP/Kate Brumback)

ATHENS, Ga. (AP) -- As college students return to campus in Georgia, a new state policy has closed the doors of the five most competitive state schools to Illegal Immigrants, but a group of professors has found a way to offer those students a taste of what they've been denied.

Five University of Georgia professors have started a program they're calling Freedom University. They're offering to teach a rigorous seminar course once a week meant to mirror courses taught at the most competitive schools and aimed at students who have graduated from high school but can't go to one of those top schools because of the new policy.

"This is not a substitute for letting these students into UGA, Georgia State or the other schools," said Pam Voekel, a history professor at UGA and one of the program's initiators. It is designed for people who, right now, don't have another option.

The policy, adopted last fall by the university system's Board of Regents, bars any state college or university that has rejected academically qualified applicants in the previous two years from admitting illegal immigrants. Illegal immigrants may still be admitted to any other state college or university, provided that they pay out-of-state tuition. The new rule came in response to public concerns that Georgia State Colleges and Universities were being overrun by illegal immigrants, that taxpayers were subsidizing their education and that legal residents were being displaced. A study conducted by the university system's Board of Regents last year found that less than one percent of the state's public college students were illegal immigrants, and that students who pay out-of-state tuition more than pay for their education.

- "What we're hoping is that people in decision-making positions will reconsider the policy," said Reinaldo Roman, another of the organizing professors. "It goes counter to our aims. We have invested enormous resources in these young people. It makes sense to give them a chance at an education."

- For now, the course will simply serve to expose the students to a college environment and challenge them intellectually. It will not likely count for credit should the students be accepted at another school, but the professors said they're seeking accreditation so credits would be transferable at some point in the future.

- **The five founding professors all work for UGA**, but they stress that the program has no connection to the institution. UGA referred a request for comment to the Board of Regents. Regents, spokesman John Millsaps said faculty members are generally free to do whatever they want with their free time as long as it doesn't interfere with their responsibilities as employees of the university system. But he said he didn't know enough about the program to comment on this specific case.

**Once the professors hatched their plan, which was suggested by an Illegal Immigrant community member who works with a lot of illegal immigrant teens,** they reached out to professors at prestigious schools nationwide to sit on a national board of advisers. One of them is Pulitzer Prize winning author and MIT professor Junot Diaz, who calls policies barring illegal immigrants from state schools cruel and divisive. He said he's ready to help Freedom University succeed.

**With professors donating their time and a local Latino community outreach center offering a space for free, the program has few costs.** They've started an *Amazon.com* wish list asking people to donate textbooks for students and gas cards for volunteers who will drive students to and from class.

- According to Professor Diaz, "This program has proved to be highly **successful** over the last five years and today, our faculty are fully committed to providing students with college courses equivalent to those taught at the state's most selective universities. In addition, we provide college application and scholarship assistance, leadership development, and movement skill-building to empower a new generation of undocumented youth leaders. We believe that all human beings -- regardless of race, ethnicity, class, religion, gender, sexual orientation, or citizenship status -- have a universal right to education.

- **As a result of our work, one out of every five students that walks into Freedom University banned from public higher education in Georgia leaves with a full merit scholarship to a college out of state.**

- **As a result of our collaboration with the Freedom at Emory Initiative,** Emory University announced in April 2015, that it would accept qualified undocumented students and provide privately-funded, need-based financial aid to those who qualify. We are building a powerful documented undocumented student movement that will win fair admissions policies in Georgia and give rise to a new generation of movement leaders."

- DACA Students filed a lawsuit in 2015 to attempt to overturn the Georgia Board of Regents policy. However, after losing two appeals, the Georgia Supreme Court finally ruled on February 1, 2016, upholding the lower Courts' decisions to dismiss the DACA Students lawsuit on grounds of immunity. All state governments and agencies are protected from being sued under the doctrine of sovereign immunity and the case was dismissed.

Adding insult-to-injury, the same Georgia Board of Regents allows the College of Coastal Georgia to offer In-state Tuition Waivers to out-of-state neighboring Students under the assumption that it increases diversity opportunities. This same Board has identified fifteen other Georgia Colleges,mostly South Georgia, although there are three or four in the metro Atlanta area according to an *AJC* report by Janel Davis, that due to declined enrollments, are being approved to offer In-State Tuition Waivers to Out-of-State neighboring students as well.

Georgia and most other States are grappling with Hispanics leading the charge of the transformative colorization of this Nation and the undeniable achievement gap.

- How sensible is it to continue to deny an essential segment of your prospective future workforce an opportunity to earn a College Degree and help your economy grow?

- As the percentage of White students shrinks and the percentage of students of color grow, the U.S. will be left with an education system that doesn't serve the majority of its children properly. The Gaps in Education will prove especially problematic unless we can all see and move beyond *xenophobia* permanently.

### *Summation:*

The Minority-Majority transformation for all U.S. school age children is already in effect and will completely manifest in 2018. All 50 States in the U.S. are equally experiencing the ill-effects of this first-time demographic shift that will have a profound impact on their socioeconomic sustainability going forward, **thus determining the future economic stability of this once great nation.**

- You can't have an effective Economic System where fewer and fewer People participate. US CAPITALISM IS DESTROYING ITSELF.

# Illiteracy:

Another under reported challenge to minorities and disadvantaged youths and adults in the U.S. is that while the media focuses more on the U.S.'s current **49 *million citizens*** (majority minority) ***in poverty,*** illiteracy **may pose a bigger threat;** **14%** or ***32 million people are illiterate.***

- 25% of U.S. children grow up illiterate.
- Students who don't read proficiently by third grade are four times more likely to drop out of school.
- 70% of students who can't read proficiently by the end of fourth grade end up in jail or on welfare.
- 70% of prisoners can't read.
- 21% of adults read below the fifth grade level.
- 19% of high school graduates in this country can't read.
- America is the only free-market OECD (Organization for Cooperation and Development) where the current generation is less educated than the previous one.

## *Case in Point:*

**I have experienced firsthand what adult illiteracy looks like** through volunteering as an adult illiteracy instructor during my graduate studies at Webster University in St. Louis, Missouri. That was a life-changing experience which opened my eyes to the extent of this sensitive challenge many of our fellow **Americans** face in their daily lives.

**In this role**, I taught adults ranging from 18 to 65. The most profound characteristic they all shared in common was not the fact that they were all illiterate, but the mere fact that they were all ashamed and very insecure about their circumstances. Through my compassion to help and my passion to empower them, I was able to establish rapport and begin to understand each person's journey. This allowed me to craft a tailored literacy plan for each individual.

**I came to understand** that each had developed their own personalized system of learning to read through various techniques of learning to identify words through site, symbols, and signs. To the average person, you would never be able to detect that a person can't read unless they were reading aloud or you were reading aloud along with them, discovering that they lacked basic phonic skills necessary to attack and breakdown new words. I also discovered that most were gainfully employed, but had finally realized that in order to secure a promotion or advance their careers, they would have to learn to read, in order to begin to complete their GED requirements. This was the single most important reason for enrolling in my class.

- I'm proud to say that 90% of all students enrolled learned to read. However,I was most disappointed with the 10% who simply gave up and dropped out.

## *Case in Point:*

I remember growing up as an inquisitive teenager, reading and hearing about the terrible **Cuban Crisis** and how their support of Russia and Communism posed a direct threat to Americas' security and how bad and how much of a tyrant **Fidel Castro** was. Trust me, I am not a supporter of Communism at all, but I do believe in giving credit where credit is due.

History has taught me that for all of the alleged bad, evil, and terrible things that have been associated with **Fidel Castro**, I discovered that one of the most empowering and definitive leadership campaigns he successfully accomplished for the Citizens of Cuba was the fact that once he took control of the country, **he ensured that every citizen of Cuba would become literate by waging a National Literacy Campaign.**

- This campaign was highly successful and innovative whereby every literate citizen was recruited and called to action, from as young as twelve to infinity. Groups traversed across the entire country teaching their fellow Cubans how to read and achieved 100% success.

I am totally convinced that there is no morally acceptable reason why thirty-two million of our fellow Americans are allowed to remain in this state of disadvantage, illiterate. For every one we leave behind, limits our full capacity to grow forward.

## Youth Homelessness:

In the U.S.today, according to the National Coalition for the Homeless there exist approximately **3.5 million homeless citizens** in America on any given night. According to an American Institutes for Research Study, **71%** or **2.5 Million** are youth age 18 or younger which represents yet another **American tragedy** that tears at the core of her conflicted values. In the 2012 - 13 School Year, *a record high 1.2 million U.S. children* in **Public Pre-Kindergarten and K-12 were homeless.** This is an increase of 8% from the previous year. Most live with friends or extended family; 16% or 192,000 live in shelters, 3% or 36,000 live without any shelter, and 6% or 72,000 live without any adult supervision. As expected, their learning and academic performance is negatively compromised. Only **47%** are proficient in reading and **44%** in math. *How did we get here?*

- The majority of homeless teens are runaways from home (1 of 7 U.S.children will run away from home by age 18).
- 50% of teens aging out of foster care or released from juvenile detention will become homeless.
- 75% of runaways are females.
- 80% resort to drugs and alcohol to cope with their trauma.
- 40% are Lesbian, Bisexual, Gay, Trans-gender (LBGT). 58% have been sexually victimized.
- 75% of all homeless youth perform below grade level in reading.
- 75% of homeless teens 16 or older drop out of school.

They all lack the major thing that most human's desire…stability.

There are many theories and reasons social scientists have suggested as root causes for this new and growing phenomenon, but one thing is apparently clear, if we choose not to address this dire moral challenge by continuing to allow it to fester, it will effectively constrain one of our most valuable youthful *resource pools* for which we all shall share in its *economic shortcomings.*

The vast majority of youth do not become homeless by choice. Various studies have suggested that the primary reasons are family dysfunction, sexual abuse, aging out of the Foster Care System, exiting the Juvenile Justice System, and economic hardship.

The two most prevalent federal programs providing assistance to homeless youth in America are chronically underfunded:

- **The Runaway and Homeless Youth Act** (RHYA) has never budgeted more than **$115 million** since inception, funding authority for all types of outreach, basic centers, and transitional living programs nationwide. With 2.5 million homeless youth, this equates to a disgraceful budget of only $46.00 per person. Truly, it is a socioeconomic necessity to do more.

- **The McKinney-Vento Homeless Assistance Act**, a HUD administered program, is only appropriated at **$65 million** per year to ensure equal access to education (including transportation) to and from school. Given that public education supports approximately 1.2 million of the total 2.5 million homeless youth; this averages out to **$54.00** per youth per year. No comment necessary. This is atrocious.

America, if we endeavor to continue to practice our current state of collective delusion in regards to this very real and threatening youth homelessness crisis, it will prove to have the same effect as if the IRS suddenly placed a tax lien on your bank account to collect taxes in support of a specific Government budget shortfall unannounced.

*"We can all endeavor to volunteer to help now or be forced to support them later."*

# Chapter 10

# Labor Crisis or Immigration Exploitation

*Corporate capitalism will always pursue the lowest cost supplier…always.*

## Manufacturing Labor Shift (Outsourcing):

**AS THE RESULT OF GLOBALIZATION** during the late 1990's, the U.S. began heavily outsourcing millions of low-skilled manufacturing jobs overseas due to cheaper labor costs. From 2000 to 2014, the U.S.lost in excess of five million manufacturing jobs to China, Mexico, and Japan. From 1999 to 2011, **China** alone secured **2.4 million** of these jobs due to extremely low labor rates of **$1.00/hour**. Today, even China is starting to lose low-skilled manufacturing jobs to poorer countries such as **Bangladesh** and **Vietnam with labor rates of $0.43 and $0.11 per hour, respectively.** As more Third World Countries continue to develop, the battle for economic development and job creation becomes more and more paramount.

## Exploitation of Prison Labor—*Twenty-first Century Peonage*

According to an *Alternet* article, "21st Century Slaves: How Corporations Exploit Prison Labor," published July 11, 2011, and the *Atlantic* "Prison Labor in America", published September 21, 2015; the U.S. Prison population in 2014 stood at roughly **2.2 million** (up **296%** from 744,000 in 1995) of which 80% is comprised predominantly of black and hispanic male inmates who earn on average **$0.25/hour**, yet cost the average taxpayer **$31,296/ per year** or about **$40 billion per year**. Although the U.S. represents only **5%** of the world's population, it houses **25%** of the prison population.

The prison industry complex is *one of the fastest-growing industries ($57 Billion) in the United States.* This multibillion-dollar industry has its own trade exhibitions, conventions, websites, and mail-order/Internet catalogs. It also has direct advertising campaigns, architecture companies, construction companies, investment houses on Wall Street, plumbing supply companies, food supply companies, armed security, and padded cells in a large variety of colors.

The prison privatization boom began in the 1980s, under the governments of Ronald Reagan and Bush Sr., but reached its height in 1990 under William Clinton when Wall Street stocks were selling like hotcakes. Clinton's program for cutting the federal workforce resulted in the Justice Department contracting with private prison corporations for the incarceration of undocumented workers and high-security inmates.

Corrections Corporation of America (CCA) and The GEO Group are the most well-known and profitable private prison operators in the U.S. who had combined revenues of about **$3.3 Billion** in 2014. These two companies dominate the market and have so much political clout and leverage that they now are in position to negotiate with State governors nationwide to **guarantee minimum occupancy rates of 90%** throughout **the contract term** prior to agreeing to take over management of existing facilities or construction of new facilities, almost monopolistic.

According to the *Left Business Observer* 2015 Report, the Federal prison industry produces **100%** of all military helmets, ammunition belts, bullet-proof vests, ID tags, shirts, pants, tents, bags, and canteens. Along with war supplies, prison workers supply **98%** of the entire market for equipment assembly services; **93%** of paints and paintbrushes**; 92%**of stove assembly; **46%**of body armor; **36%** of home appliances; **30%** of headphones, microphones, speakers; and **21%** of office furniture, as well as airplane parts, medical supplies, and much more. Prisoners are even raising seeing-eye dogs for blind people.

## Manufacturing (Reshoring)

Thanks to prison labor, the United States is once again an attractive location for investment in manufacturing work that was designed for third world labor markets. A company that operated a Maquiladora, an assembly plant in Mexico near the border, closed down its operations there and relocated to San Quentin State Prison in California. In Texas, a factory fired its 150 workers and contracted the services of prisoner-workers from the private Lockhart, Texas prison where circuit boards are assembled for companies like IBM and Compaq…"Peonage Redux."

Who is investing? **At least thirty-seven states have legalized the contracting of prison labor by private corporations** that mount their operations inside state prisons. The list of such companies contains the cream of U.S. corporate society: IBM, Boeing, Motorola, Microsoft, AT&T, Wireless, Texas Instrument, Dell, Compaq, Honeywell, Hewlett-Packard, Nortel, Lucent Technologies, 3Com, Intel, Northern Telecom, TWA, Nordstrom, Revlon, Macy's, Pierre Cardin, Target Stores, and many more. All of these businesses are excited about the **economic boom generated by prison labor**. Between 1980 and 1994, profits went up from $392 million to $1.31 billion. Inmates in state penitentiaries generally receive the minimum wage for their work, but not all. In Colorado, they get about $2 per hour, well under the minimum. And in privately run prisons, they receive as little as **17 cents** per hour for a maximum of six hours a day. The equivalent of **$20 per month.** The highest-paying private prison is CCA in Tennessee, where prisoners receive **50 cents per hour** for what they call highly skilled positions. At those rates, it is no surprise that inmates find the pay in federal prisons to be very generous. There, they can earn $1.25 an hour and work eight hours a day, and sometimes overtime. They can send home $200 - $300 per month.

- Nike was lured by the governor of Oregon to relocate its manufacturing facility from Indonesia to Oregon's Prison System which guaranteed cheaper prison labor cost.

This is CORPRATE WELFARE at its finest. It is so profitable many are calling it the *"New Indentured Servitude." It's merely a reincarnation of Peonage.*

This is Corporate Socialism and Capitalism working hand-to-mouth. With the private prison management companies also known as government tcontractors and Fortune 500 partners reaping 99% of the benefits and profits in excess of $40 Billion/Year at the expense of the

Indentured Servants (Inmates) and the bondage of U.S. taxpayers who are taxed at $40 Billion/Year.

## *Recidivism*

According to a National Institute of Justice Report dated June 17, 2014, within three years of release, about two-thirds (**67.8%**) of released prisoners were rearrested. Within five years of release, about three-quarters (**76.6%**) of released prisoners were rearrested. Of those prisoners who were rearrested, more than half (**56.7%**), were arrested by the end of the first year.

- Consider that **95%** of those incarcerated will be released at some point and that we will continue to be forced to take care of them one way or another, through public benefits or through future incarceration.

- The only solution in ending the exploitation of recidivism is prison system reform.

## Global Capitalism and Immigrant Labor (21st Century Slavery):

According to a *Take Part Organization* article, the larger story behind immigration reform is capitalist globalization and the worldwide reorganization of the system for supplying labor to the global economy. Over the past few decades there has been an upsurge in transnational migration as every country and region has become integrated, often violently, into global capitalism through foreign invasions, occupations, free trade agreements, neo-liberal social and economic policies, and financial crisis. Hundreds of millions have been displaced from the countryside in the Global South and turned into internal and transnational migrants, providing a vast new pool of exploitable labor for the global economy as national labor markets have increasingly merged into a global labor market.

The creation of immigrant labor pools is a worldwide phenomenon, in which poles of accumulation in the global economy attract immigrant labor from their peripheries. Thus, to name a few of the major twenty-first century transnational labor flows, Turkish and Eastern European workers supply labor to Western Europe, Central Africans to South

Africa, Nicaraguans to Costa Rica, Sri Lanka and other South Asians to the Middle East oil producing countries, Asians to Australia, Thais to Japan, Indonesians to Malaysia, and so on. In all of these cases, it is repressive state controls that create immigrant workers as a distinct category of labor that becomes central to the whole global capitalist economy. As borders have come down for capital and goods, they have been reinforced for human beings. A recent survey by *TakePart. com* reveals that 1 out of every 122 humans worldwide is now either a refugee, internally displaced, or seeking asylum. That's roughly 59.5 million people. These numbers are the highest since records have been kept. Most are fleeing from conflict, poverty, or oppression. While global capitalism creates immigrant workers, these workers do not enjoy citizenship rights in their host countries. Stripped either de facto or de jure of the political, civic, and labor rights afforded to citizens, immigrant workers are forced into the underground, made vulnerable to employers, whether large private, state employers or affluent. They are subjected to hostile cultural and ideological environments. Neither employers, nor, state governments want to do away with immigrant labor. To the contrary, they want to sustain a vast exploitable labor pool that exists under precarious conditions that is flexible and disposable through deportation and therefore controllable. This super-exploitation of an immigrant workforce would not be possible if that workforce had the same civil, political and labor rights as citizens, if it did not face the insecurities and vulnerabilities of being undocumented or illegal.

Driving immigrant labor underground and absolving the state and employers of any commitment to the social reproduction of this labor allows for its maximum exploitation together with its disposal when necessary. In this way the immigrant labor force becomes responsible for its own maintenance and reproduction and also through remittances for their family members abroad. This makes immigrant labor low-cost and flexible for capital *and also* costless for the state compared to native born labor.

In summation, the division of the global working class into citizen and immigrant is a major new axis of inequality worldwide. Borders and nationality are used by transnational capital, the powerful and the privileged, to sustain new methods of control and domination over the global working class.

**HUMANITARIANISM IS NON-PARTISAN.**

## U.S. Capitalism of Immigrant Labor:

The U.S. economy has become increasingly dependent on immigrant labor. There are an estimated 34 million immigrants in the United States, 20 million of these from Latin America, and 11 to 12 million undocumented, most of them of Latin American origin. This is, however, a contradictory situation. From the viewpoint of the dominant groups, the dilemma is how to super-exploit an immigrant labor force, such as Latinos in the U.S., yet how to simultaneously assure it is super controllable and super-controlled. The push in the United States and elsewhere has been towards heightened criminalization of immigrant communities, the militarized control of these communities, and the establishment of an immigrant detention and deportation complex... stealinglives.

*"It's not by force alone that man finds his reward."*

## The immigrant military-prison-industrial-detention complex:

But there is another less evident dimension to the criminalization of immigrants and the militarized control of their communities and the border. The immigrant military-prison-industrial-detention complex is one of the fastest growing sectors of the U.S. economy. There has been a boom in new private prison construction to house immigrants detained during deportation proceedings. In 2007, nearly one million undocumented immigrants were apprehended and 311,000 deported. The Obama administration presents itself as a friend of Latinos and immigrants, in general. Yet, Obama has deported more immigrants than any other president in the past half a century, some 400,000 per year since he took office in 2009.

Immigrant labor is extremely profitable for the corporate economy in double sense. First, as noted, it is labor that is highly vulnerable, forced to exist semi-underground, and deportable, and therefore super-exploitable. Second, the criminalization of undocumented immigrants and the militarization of their control, not only reproduce the opportunity to exploit them, but also allows for mass labor accumulation.

The private immigrant detention complex is a boom industry. Undocumented immigrants constitute the fastest growing sector of the U.S. prison population and are detained in private detention centers and deported by private companies contracted out by the U.S. As of 2010, there were 270 immigration detention centers that caged on any given day over 30,000 immigrants. Since detainment facilities and deportation logistics are subcontracted to private companies, capital has a vested interest in the criminalization of immigrants and in the militarization of control over immigrants and more broadly, therefore, a vested interest in contributing to the neo-fascist anti-immigrant movement.

It is no surprise that William Andrews, the CEO of the Corrections Corporation of America, or CCA, the largest private U.S. contractor for immigrant detention centers, declared in 2008, "the demand for our facilities and services could be adversely affected by the relaxation of enforcement efforts...or through decriminalization [of immigrants]." A month after the anti-immigrant bill in Arizona, SB1070, became law, Wayne Callabres, the president of Geo Group, another private prison contractor, held a conference call with investors and explained his company's aspirations. "Opportunities at the federal level are going to continue apace as a result of what's happening," he said, referring to the Arizona law. "Those people coming across the border being caught are going to have to be detained and that to me at least suggests there's going to be enhanced opportunities for what we do...stealing lives.

## Containing the Immigrant Rights Movement

The war on terror paved the way for an undeclared war on immigrants by fusing national security and anti-terrorism with immigration law enforcement, involving designation of borders and immigrant flows as terrorism threats. There has been approval of vast new funding and the passage of a slew of policies and laws to undertake the new war. This war has further escalated in response to the spread worldwide of an immigrant rights movement to fightback against repression, exploitation, exclusion, cultural degradation and racism. A major turning point in this struggle in the United States came in spring 2006 with a series of unparalleled strikes and demonstrations that swept the country. The immediate trigger for these mass protests was the introduction in the U.S. Congress of a bill known as the Sensenbrenner bill that called for criminalizing undocumented immigrants by making it a felony to be in the U.S. without proper documentation. It also stipulated construction of a militarized wall between Mexico and the U.S. and the application of criminal sanctions against anyone who provided assistance to undocumented immigrants, including churches, humanitarian groups, and social service agencies. The protests defeated the Sensenbrenner bill and at the same time frightened the ruling class, sparking an escalation of state repression and racist nativism and fueled the neo-fascist anti-immigrant movement. The backlash involved, among other things, stepped-up raids on immigrant workplaces and communities, mass deportations, an increase in the number of federal immigration enforcement agents, the deputizing of local police forces as enforcement agents, the further militarization of the U.S.-Mexico border, anti-immigrant hysteria in the mass media, and the introduction at local, state, and federal levels of a slew of discriminatory anti-immigrant legislative initiatives. Lifting national borders for capital and simultaneously reinforcing these same national boundaries is a contradictory situation that helps generate a nationalist hysteria by propagating such images as out of control borders and invasions of illegal immigrants. Racist hostility towards Latinos and other immigrants may be intentionally generated by right-wing politicians, law-enforcement agents and neo-fascist anti-immigrant movements. They may be the effect of the structural and legalinstitutional subordination of immigrant workers and their communities, or simply an unintended (although not necessarily unwelcomed) byproduct of the state's coercive policies.

## The crisis, cooptation, and reform legislation:

White middle and world class sectors in the U.S. faced downward mobility and heightened insecurities as the welfare state and job stability have been dismantled in the face of capitalist globalization. These sectors have been particularly prone to being organized into racist anti-immigrant politics by conservative political groups housed inside and outside of the Republican Party. Anti-immigrant forces have tried to draw in White workers with appeals to racial solidarity and to xenophobia and scapegoating of immigrant communities.

It is widely recognized that Obama's 2012 reelection hinged heavily on the Latino vote, and that this voting block is expanding rapidly, something that has caused important sectors of the Republican Party to reconsider immigration reform. It may be that the 2012 vote gave the necessary impetus to bringing together a critical mass around the reformation of the strategy and methods for reproducing and controlling a reserve army of immigrant labor.

The reform legislation passed in the Senate on June 27, 2013, meets the interests of the immigrant military-prison-industrial-detention complex. Military contractors, Silicon Valley, law enforcement, construction and private prison companies stand to earn billions in profits. Agribusiness and the corporate sector will continue to exploit a largely captive labor force, racialized and relegated to second class status, especially among the millions of immigrants who will be unable to legalize their status, among new immigrants, and among those brought in as guest workers. It is no wonder that along with corporate lobbyists staunch anti-immigrant conservatives such as Arizona governor Jan Brewer, FOX News commentator Bill O'Reilly, and Tea Party icon Rand Paul, have endorsed the bill. The House is divided over this bill and has delayed their decision indefinitely.

As a result, on November 20, 2014, the President announced a series of Executive Actions to crack down on

illegal immigration at the border, prioritize deporting felons not families, and require certain undocumented immigrants to pass a criminal background check and pay taxes in order to temporarily stay in the U.S. without fear of deportation.

## These initiatives include:

- Expanding the population eligible for the Deferred Action for Childhood Arrivals (DACA) program to people of any current age who entered the United States before the age of 16 and lived intheUnited States continuously since January 1, 2010, and extending the period of DACA and work authorization from two years to three years.

- Allowing parents of U.S. citizens and lawful permanent residents to request deferred action and employment authorization for three years, in a new Deferred Action for Parents of Americans and Lawful Permanent Residents program, provided they have lived in the United States continuously since January 1, 2010, and pass required background checks.

- Expanding the use of provisional waivers of unlawful presence to include the spouses and sons and daughters of lawful permanent residents and the sons and daughters of U.S. citizens.

- Modernizing, improving and clarifying immigrant and nonimmigrant visa programs to grow our economy and create jobs.

- Promoting citizenship education and public awareness for lawful permanent residents and providing an option for naturalization applicants to use credit cards to pay the application fee.

Subject Executive Orders were rejected by the U.S. Appeals Court 5th District on November 15, 2015, and are currently under consideration to be heard in the U.S. Supreme Court in 2016.

*"HUMANITARIANISM IS NON-PARTISAN."*

# Chapter 11

# Our Valley of Solidarity

*In order for us to create a better society, we first must endeavor to understand the most pressing and inequitable challenges that continue to enslave us in the "**Valley**" by identifying and surveying these issues, then committing to eradicating and liberating ourselves from them collectively.*

## Our Biggest Challenge

**CONTINUE TO CREATE ENDLESS DEBT AND SOCIAL DISTRUST;** Would we prefer the Government to continue to create **endless debt** in its frugal attempt to support and fund our growing social service obligations to include Medicare, Medicaid, Food Stamps, Prisons/Incarceration Housing, Mental Health, Education, Corporate Welfare, new Affordable Healthcare Plans, etc.? Our continuous glorifying of sinful acts of "***xenophobic delusion***" divides us racially, economically, religiously, and socially beyond measure.

OR

**Create a Better Society:** This can be done by committing to a rededication of solidarity, accepting, respecting, and lifting each other up, increasing federal minimum wage rates, eliminating welfare, creating a more effective and efficient education system at every level, lowering crime rates, lowering incarceration through devising better intervention programs, eradicating poverty, illiteracy, homelessness, increasing high school and college graduation rates, and encouraging job participation through creating more corporate partnerships, promoting co-op and apprenticeship programs, and devising more conducive corporate and individual tax strategies. *See and move beyond our current "xenophobic society to a Nation of solidarity."*

# VALLEY

Valley is a place, period, or situation filled with fear and gloom. The views are very restrictive and add to our distress; whether priest or pagan, rich or poor, Black or White, male or female, VALLEY TIMES come to us all.

*Believers tend to think that their faith will deflect hard times…de*lusional.

Our hearts are especially consoled when someone volunteers to GO INTO THE VALLEY WITH us.

## Men of The Valley

**Priests** are known as MEN OF THE VALLEY who carry out repairs of suffering souls;"After him, the priests, the Men of the Valley, carried out repairs" (Nehemiah 3:22 NASB).We too, as believers, should learn to practice humility and choose to serve our brothers and sisters who face hardships in the valley.

Many charismatic religious leaders pervert the gospel for profit instead of becoming rich in the gospel which promises eternal profits.

### *Case in Point:*
The following insightful story is an excerpt from the book – "***Hearts That We Broke Long Ago***" by *Merele Shaine:*

And the Lord said to the Rabbi, "come, I will show you **Hell**."

They entered a room where a group of people sat around a huge pot of stew. Everyone was famished and desperate. Each held a spoon that reached the pot, but had a handle so long that it could not be used to reach their mouths – The suffering was terrible.

"Come, now I will show you **Heaven**," the Lord said after a while.

They entered another room, identical to the first – the pot of stew, the group of people, the same long spoons.

But, there, everyone was happy and well nourished.

"I don't understand," said the Rabbi. "Why are they happy here when they were miserable in the other room, and everything looks the same?"

The Lord smiled, "Ah, but don't you see? *Here they have learned to feed each other.*"

## Religious Disorder:

The single most segregated institution in the U.S. today is churches and houses of worship, whereby

most have remained consistently segregated by race and the shameful practice of xenophobia is more subtle.

- "Religious preferences today have been marginalized to the extent of being nothing more than a separate Spiritual Designer Label."

## Poverty:

In 2013, according to the U.S. Census Bureau, the U.S. spent $1 trillion or $21,700 per citizen on Anti-Poverty programs to include Temporary Assistance for Needy Families (TANF), Medicaid Food Stamps, and WIC citizens received these benefits. The 2013 census further stated that there are 109,631,000 citizens near poverty, plus an additional 49 Million in poverty or a total of 158,631,000 U.S. citizens receiving social welfare assistance, yet there only exist 122,000,000 full time year-round employees in the U.S. which equates to 36,631,000 more citizens receiving Government poverty benefits than the total fully employed U.S. workforce.

- Every American family that pays its own way, and takes care of its own children, whether with one or two incomes – must subsidize the 158,631,000 in-or-near-poverty. One of three children live in poverty, and the numbers are growing.In spite of this huge financial burden placed on the average American citizen, results have been minimal. The additional 109,631,000 people classified as the working poor also known as the near poverty,; work full-time jobs where their income is so low, it qualifies them as poor according to Government poverty guidelines which permits them to qualify for Government Welfare Assistance. This has resulted in 159,000,000 or approximately 50% of the total U.S. population receiving federal assistance, compared to 60 million or14.29% of the U.S. population in1935 that were on welfare.

The more the U.S. grows, the more poverty we create; the society becomes debased and fosters a sense of helplessness, lowering the quality of life and value for the masses.

• Poverty is a byproduct of distrust. If people don't trust the system, if they think society is lying to them when it tells them that discipline and hard work will be rewarded, if they don't think people like them can really make it, they have no real incentive to aspire to greatness.

NOTHING brings as much suffering and humility as POVERTY. Only those who have experienced it understand.

• Material success creates Social Failure. Unequal societies are bad for everyone, the well-off and the poor.

• Individualism in the pursuit of happiness has failed - *The American dream is a myth.*

• Social work and reform may eliminate certain forms of suffering and injustice, but they are only temporary and can never cure the torment of men's souls, nor bring them into the eternal relationship with God.

The U.S. poverty rate has increased by more than 266% from 1935 to 2015. We're headed down the wrong road...poverty is slavery.

## Education

In 2013, according to the U.S. Department of Education, the U.S. spent $174 billion on Federal College Financial Aid with seemingly dismal results, considering that while most Colleges and Universities have been able to increase their enrollments, graduation rates have continued to decline. Only 47.9% of all eligible U.S. high school students attend College in the U.S. In spite of this tremendous investment, the U.S., who once set the benchmark of being the world's most educated society, now ranks fourteenth and dropping like a bullet.

• Community Colleges educate 44% of all U.S. undergraduate students, but only 39% graduate.

- National Institutional data show that students testing below ninth grade level English and Math enrolling in College Developmental Studies Courses are highly unlikely to qualify for degree status.

In 2014, only 23% of Black Students attended majority White Public Schools which is exactly the same as in 1968. The remaining 77% of Black school aged kids attend predominantly Minority-Majority Schools, while 80% of Latino children attend Minority-Majority schools.

*Many of our youth today regard academic superiority as a social liability.*

*An uneducated nation shall never prosper.*

# THE GREAT ESCAPE – XEN CITIES

## *The Most Diverse Cities Are Often the Most Segregated*

According to a startling report published in *Urban Diversity* onMay 1, 2015, by Nate Silver data drawn from the Brown University American Communities Project, which is in turn, based on the 2010 Census. Brown's data defines five racial groups: Whites, Blacks, Hispanics, Asians and other, where other principally refers to Native Americans. The groups are exhaustive, meaning they add up to 100 percent of the population and mutually exclusive (they don't overlap).

### The Most Diverse And Most Segregated Cities
Among 100 most populous U.S. cities

| | CITYWIDE DIVERSITY INDEX | | | NEIGHBORHOOD DIVERSITY INDEX | | | INTEGRATION / SEGREGATION INDEX | |
|---|---|---|---|---|---|---|---|---|
| | Most diverse at city level | | | Most diverse at neighborhood level | | | Most integrated | |
| 1 | Jersey City, NJ | 75.5% | 1 | Sacramento, CA | 66.5% | 1 | Irvine, CA | +11.0% |
| 2 | Oakland, CA | 74.8 | 2 | Stockton, CA | 64.3 | 2 | Sacramento, CA | +10.1 |
| 3 | Sacramento, CA | 73.8 | 3 | Jersey City, NJ | 63.4 | 3 | Paradise, NV | +9.8 |
| 4 | New York, NY | 73.3 | 4 | N. Las Vegas, NV | 61.8 | 4 | Stockton, CA | +9.2 |
| 5 | Stockton, CA | 71.6 | 5 | Garland, TX | 61.7 | 5 | Fremont, CA | +8.8 |
| 6 | Long Beach, CA | 70.5 | 6 | Paradise, NV | 61.6 | 6 | Chula Vista, CA | +8.7 |
| 7 | Chicago, IL | 70.3 | 7 | Oakland, CA | 60.7 | 7 | Anchorage, AK | +8.4 |
| 8 | N. Las Vegas, NV | 70.2 | 8 | Irving, TX | 59.8 | 8 | Henderson, NV | +8.3 |
| 9 | Irving, TX | 69.9 | 9 | Aurora, CO | 59.5 | 9 | Garland, TX | +8.3 |
| 10 | San Jose, CA | 69.1 | 10 | Arlington, TX | 58.9 | 10 | Aurora, CO | +8.0 |
| | Least diverse at city level | | | Least diverse at neighborhood level | | | Most segregated | |
| 1 | Laredo, TX | 8.4% | 1 | Laredo, TX | 8.2% | 1 | Chicago, IL | -18.6% |
| 2 | Hialeah, FL | 10.1 | 2 | Hialeah, FL | 10.0 | 2 | Atlanta, GA | -14.5 |
| 3 | Scottsdale, AZ | 28.9 | 3 | Detroit, MI | 17.8 | 3 | Milwaukee, WI | -13.1 |
| 4 | Detroit, MI | 29.0 | 4 | Birmingham, AL | 26.7 | 4 | Philadelphia, PA | -12.6 |
| 5 | Lincoln, NE | 30.1 | 5 | Scottsdale, AZ | 27.2 | 5 | St. Louis, MO | -11.3 |
| 6 | El Paso, TX | 32.8 | 6 | Lincoln, NE | 28.5 | 6 | Washington, DC | -11.1 |
| 7 | Santa Ana, CA | 36.7 | 7 | Miami, FL | 28.6 | 7 | Baltimore, MD | -11.1 |
| 8 | Honolulu, HI | 40.5 | 8 | El Paso, TX | 29.0 | 8 | Baton Rouge, LA | -11.0 |
| 9 | Madison, WI | 40.9 | 9 | Baltimore, MD | 29.5 | 9 | Cleveland, OH | -10.9 |
| 10 | Birmingham, AL | 41.0 | 10 | Atlanta, GA | 30.7 | 10 | New Orleans, LA | -10.2 |

FIVETHIRTYEIGHT    BASED ON DATA FROM BROWN UNIVERSITY'S AMERICAN COMMUNITIES PROJECT

The Most Diverse Cities are often the Most Segregated cities.You can have a diverse city, but not diverse neighborhoods. Whereas Chicago's citywide diversity index is 70%, seventh best out of the 100 most populous U.S. cities, its neighborhood diversity index is just 36%, which ranks 82nd. New York also has a big gap. Its citywide diversity index is 73%, fourth highest in the country, but its neighborhood diversity index is 47%, which ranks 49th.

Cities with substantial Black populations tend to be highly segregated. Of the top 100 U.S. cities by population, thirty-five are at least one-quarter black, and only six of those cities have positive integration scores. Most cities east of the Rocky Mountains with substantial Black populations are quite segregated. There's not a lot to distinguish Baltimore from Cleveland, Memphis, Milwaukee, New Orleans, Philadelphia or St. Louis.

- One amazing observation in regards to these undisputable truths is that although the **City of Atlanta**, Georgia, being named the **number two most segregated City in America,** was awarded a new MLS Soccer Franchise in 2015 and had the **audacity to name it Atlanta United**. How pathetic.

- Atlanta also ranked **number 3** nationwide in **income inequality** in 2016, according to the Atlanta Journal Constitution.

## Corporate Inversions:

According to a very insightful *Bloomberg Business News 2015* article – U.S.companies are stashing **$2.1 trillion overseas to avoid taxes**. The article shed light on this growing corporate tax-avoidance strategy that seriously threatens the U.S. Tax System survivability exponentially. Many U.S. corporations use offshore tax havens and other accounting gimmicks to avoid paying as much as **$90 billion a year** in federal income taxes, also known as Corporate Inversion. A large loophole at the heart of the U.S. tax law enables corporations to avoid paying taxes on foreign profits until they are brought home. Known as deferral, it provides a huge incentive to keep profits offshore as long as possible. Many corporations choose never to bring the profits home and never pay U.S. taxes on them. Deferral gives corporations enormous incentives to use accounting tricks to make it appear that profits earned here were generated in a tax haven. Profits are funneled through subsidiaries, often shell companies with few employees and little real business activity.

A U.S. corporation can execute an inversion by buying a foreign firm and then claiming that the new, merged company is foreign. This lets it reincorporate in a country, often a tax haven, with a much lower tax rate. The process takes place on paper. The company doesn't move its headquarters offshore and its ownership is mostly unchanged. But, it continues to enjoy the privileges of operating here while paying low tax rates in the foreign country. How to solve the problem? The simplest solution is to end deferral. Corporations would pay taxes on offshore income the year it is earned, rather than indefinitely avoid paying U.S. income taxes. U.S. corporations hold $2.1 trillion in profits offshore – much in tax havens – that have not been taxed in the U.S. General Electric, which uses a loophole for offshore financial profits, earned $27.5 billion in profits from 2008 to 2012 but claimed tax refunds of $3.1 billion. Apple made $74 billion from 2009 to 2012 on worldwide sales (excluding the Americas) and paid almost nothing in taxes to any country. Twenty-six profitable Fortune 500 firms paid no federal income taxes from 2008 to 2012. One hundred-eleven large, profitable corporations paid zero federal income taxes in at least one of those five years. Corporations don't just want to defer paying U.S. taxes on foreign profits, they *want a territorial tax system* that eliminates all U.S. taxation of offshore profits. This would provide even more incentives for corporations to shift profits to offshore tax havens. A system in which U.S. corporations pay no U.S. income taxes on offshore profits would encourage U.S. firms to create 800,000 jobs overseas rather than in the U.S.

Corporations say our 35% corporate income tax rate is the highest in the world, which makes them uncompetitive and kills jobs. But corporations aren't paying too much in taxes. Many pay too little. The typical American family paid more income taxes in one year than General Electric and dozens of other companies paid in five years. Many large, profitable corporations pay a tax rate of less than 20%, and some pay absolutely nothing for years. The national average for corporate taxation is 11%. If corporations pay less, you will have to pay more. Corporations need to pay their fair share too.

The **Foreign Account Tax Compliance Act** was specifically created to regulate and put control mechanisms in place to position the U.S. Government via the IRS to legally tax these apparent tax evading multi-national corporations and related stakeholders', however, it will have very limited effect due to the following:

*Over half* of U.S. corporate foreign profits are now being held in tax havens, *double the share* of just twenty years ago. Yet for some of our largest corporations, according to the a 2013 Wall Street Journal report, over 75% of the cash owned by their foreign subsidiaries *remains in U.S. banks*, held in U.S. dollars or parked in U.S. government and corporate securities. Thus, they get the benefit of our national security while they eagerly avoid taxes.

*Wall Street Journal - "Firms Keep Stockpiles of 'Foreign' Cash in U.S."* by KATE LINEBAUGH.

There's a funny thing about the estimated $2.1 trillion that American companies say they have indefinitely invested overseas: A lot of it is actually sitting right here at home.

• Some companies, including Internet giant Google Inc., software maker Microsoft Corp. and data-storage specialist EMC Corp., keep more than three-quarters of the cash owned by their foreign subsidiaries at U.S. banks, held in U.S. dollars or parked in U.S. government and corporate securities, according to people familiar with the companies' cash positions.

In the eyes of the law, the Internal Revenue Service and Company Executives, however, this money is overseas. As long as it doesn't flow back to the U.S. parent company, the U.S. doesn't tax it. And as long as it sits in U.S. bank accounts or in U.S. Treasuries, it is safer than if it were plowed into potentially risky foreign investments.

In accounting terms, the location of the funds may be just a technicality. But for people on both sides of the contentious debate over corporate-tax reform, the situation highlights what they see as the absurdity of rules that encourage companies to engage in semantic games, legal gymnastics and inefficient corporate-financing methods to shield profits from U.S. taxes.

- Unpaid taxes of 500 Companies could pay for a job for every unemployed American for two years, in accordance with the nation's median salary of $36,000. Citizens for Tax Justice reports that Fortune 500 companies are holding over $2 trillion in profits offshore to avoid taxes that would amount to over $600 billion. Our society desperately needs infrastructure repair, but eight million potential jobs are being held hostage beyond our borders.

## The Disenfranchised – Casualties of Social Engineering:

Many of the disenfranchised Citizens of this country are minorities, who are victims of social engineering and have either, never brought into the American Dream, believe that the current power structure was never devised to serve them, or are somewhat hopeless in their future possibilities. Thus, they would continue being dependent on Government assistance for life...poverty is slavery. Ironically, the leading U.S. Economists have varying thoughts regarding the cause for the current historically low labor participation rate of 62.6%, the lowest in 37 years. However, more and more economists are leaning toward the theory of a change in attitude of how U.S. Citizens view employment in the twenty-first century. The U.S. Citizens they are referring to are middle class Americans. You can only imagine how the disenfranchised must feel. In 2015, 50% of all U.S. Citizens are in-or-near poverty, 80% of all U.S. adults are in-or-near poverty and 22% of all U.S. children live in poverty, and 49.1 million U.S. Citizens are food insecure. These historic trends are the direct result of the financial collapse of 2009 which deteriorated the American Middle Class and continues to eliminate our country'smost productive employment class. The dark shadow of slavery still permeates today and it still casts itself over every aspect of American life.

- How long will the Power Structure continue to turn a blind-eye away from the disenfranchised who have virtually been deemed invisible?*"Everyone deserves to be seen".*

## When Social Engineering Backfires:

- Wall Street has always favored poverty because they depend on cheap labor for profits. Since the Financial Crisis of 2009, the rules changed when many middle-class whites became poor, thus virtually eliminating the tax basis backbone of this Country. Corporate America only pays 11% on average of the total Government taxes collected, therefore fueling the recent debates about increasing taxes on the wealthy and Corporate America alike to close the gap vacated by the middle-class.

In 2014, a total of $1.8 trillion or 51% of the total Federal Budget was spent on Entitlement Programs to include Social Security, Medicare, and Medicaid, yet 50% of the entire U.S. population continue to live in-or-near-poverty.

Somebody please sound the alarm. We need drastic system changes now!

- With approximately 160 million U.S. citizens in-or-near-poverty, one can understand why the majority of Capitalist American employers would continue to fight against raising the minimum wage.

### *Case in Point:*

A recent Facebook post shared by a financially struggling California Customer Service Representative; shines light on this rapidly growing economic dilemma being faced by the working poor all across America:

The 25-year-old blasted her company for not paying customer service staff livable wages. "Every single one of my coworkers is struggling. They're taking side jobs. They're living at home. One of them started a GoFundMe because she couldn't pay her rent. She ended up leaving the company and moving east where minimum wages are higher.

I got paid yesterday ($733.24, bi-weekly) but I have to save as much of that as possible to pay my rent ($1245) for my apartment that's 30 miles away from work because it was the cheapest place I could find that had access to the train, which costs me $5.65 one way to get to work. That's $11.30 a day, by the way. I make $8.15 an hour after taxes.

I also have to pay my gas and electric bill. Last month it was $120 because I used my heater. I've since stopped using my heater. Have you ever slept fully clothed under several blankets just so you don't get a cold and have to miss work? Have you ever drunk a liter of water before going to bed so you could fall asleep without waking up a few hours later with stomach pains because the last time you ate was at work? I woke up today with stomach pains. I made myself a bowl of rice."

- This story echoes sentiments heard around the country over the need for a higher minimum wage.

### *Slivers of Hope: Champions of Change National Test Case:* **On June 23, 2014, the City of Seattle took the boldest stance on minimum wage in the U.S. since 1968,** when they passed legislation to raise minimum wages significantly for all employers registered within its city limits. They approved a $15 per hour minimum wage, giving its lowest-paid workers a path over the next seven years to the nation's highest hourly pay. The outcome was not in doubt as a progressive mayor and City Council throughout the spring vowed to address the national trend of rising income inequality and a city that has become increasingly unaffordable for many of its residents. Amid the celebration outside City Hall after the vote, however, cautionary notes also sounded about Seattle's leap into the unknown.

"No city or state has gone this far. We go into uncharted territory," said Seattle City Council Member Sally Clark before the council agreed to give workers a 61 percent wage increase over what is already the country's highest state minimum wage. Mayor Ed Murray praised the vote as a bold step to address what he called more than three decades of economic policy that resulted in a dismantling of the middle class. Seattle's plan actually will be phased in over a three-year period and tiered based on company type and size.

*"Today, we have taken action that will serve as a model for the rest of the nation to follow," he said.*

Kudos to the City of Seattle.

- Seattle is our undisputed choice for City Champion of Change.

As a result of Seattle's bold and compassionate courage, the following cities have followed suit:

- San Francisco passed a similar $15.00 minimum in 2014.

- In 2015, Sacramento, California, went to $12.50 and Tacoma, Washington, went to $12.While Palo Alto, California and St. Louis, Missouri, increased their wages to $11 an hour. Portland, Maine, increased its wage to $10.68, while three cities — Birmingham, Alabama; Johnson County, Iowa; and Lexington, Kentucky — all passed $10.10 wages.

- Democrats in the House and Senate have also introduced a bill in 2015 to bring the country's minimum wage up to $15.00.

## *Nation's Leading Retailer Speaks:*

**On February 15, 2015, Doug McMillon President & CEO, Walmart (America's largest Retailer)** announced that the company has agreed to raise the pay wages for 500,000 full-time and part-time associates; more than a third of its work force at Walmart (WMT) U.S. stores and Sam's Clubs, will receive pay raises in April to at least $9 an hour. That will be $1.75 above the federal minimum wage. By next February 1, 2016, their pay will go to at least $10 an hour.

Kudos to Walmart

- Walmart is our undisputed choice for Big Retail Champion of Change.

- So America, let's ask ourselves, how can Walmart, the world's largest retailer and the City of Seattle, the nation's 20th largest City/15th Metropolitan Statistical Area, demonstrate the courage and conviction to take the lead in elevating thousands of impoverished employees respectively however, our Federal Government which traditionally sets policy and takes the lead in advancing socioeconomic policies that empower and uplift the people remain silent on this issue since 1968?

It makes no economic or moral sense for the Government to continue to delay such an increase to at least $10 to $12.00 per hour considering that it would have an immediate positive impact on their Social Entitlement Budget. A great percentage of the 110 Million (In-or-Near-Poverty) current recipients would no longer qualify for such benefits. Simultaneously, these same former recipients would be elevated out of poverty…win-win for the economy.

We've come a long way, yet traveled nowhere.

The U.S. is more divided today than at any time during the twentieth century mainly due to income/wealth disparities between White, Black, and Hispanics. White wealth gap has increased by 40% since 1967. In 2013, the wealth of White households was ten times the median wealth of Black and Hispanic households respectively. Asians and other racial groups are not separately identified in the public-use versions of the Fed's survey. Segregation in Schools, Churches, and Communities is worse today than in 1965. Racism and crime against minorities has increased disproportionately. Minority incarcerations increased 269% from 1995 to 2015. White-on-Black crime has also increased disproportionately over the last fifty years. Median income for Black households is 60% of Whites. Unemployment for Blacks is 50% higher than Whites, one in four Blacks live in poverty compared to one in ten Whites, and 72% of Whites own homes compared to 43% of Black. What's even more alarming, is the fact that 40% of Blacks and Hispanics have $0.00 financial assets (excluding retirement accounts). Correcting the disparate minority education achievement gap which drives the minority wage gap must be PRIORITY number one.

*Moral obligation is required for BIG GOVERNMENT to finally stop being a Capitalism bedfellow of placing corporate policy ahead of public necessities and step down into the "Valley of Solidarity."*

The REAL problem in the U.S. is class warfare. Being poor is synonymous with being a person of color or being a criminal.

There is a Big difference between Being Poor and Living in Poverty:

• *When you are **Poor**, you still have a shot at making it. There's **HOPE**.*

• *When you live in **Poverty**, your best shot is staying alive. Life feels **HOPELESS**.*

**America today can't say it's a Land of Opportunity.** Financial Success is not a sign of virtue. It's mostly a sign that your Grandparent's did well.

# Chapter 12

# One Nation, Under God, Indivisible...

*The Pledge of Allegiance was written in August 1892 by the socialist minister Francis Bellamy (1855-1931). It was originally published in The Youth's Companion on **September 8, 1892** in celebration of the nation's first official celebration of Columbus Day. Bellamy had hoped that the pledge would be used by citizens in any country.*

## *IN ITS ORIGINAL FORM IT READ:*
*"I pledge allegiance to my Flag and the Republicfor which it stands, one nation, indivisible, with liberty and justice for all."*

*In **1923**, the words, "the Flag of the United States of America" were added. At this time it read:*

*"I pledge allegiance to the Flag of the United States of America and to the Republic for which it stands, one nation, indivisible, with liberty and justice for all."*

*In **1954,** in response to the Communist threat of the times, President Eisenhower encouraged Congress to add the words "under God," creating the 31-word pledge we say today. Bellamy's daughter objected to this alteration. Today it reads:*

**"I pledge allegiance to the flag of the United States of America, and to the republic for which it stands, one nation under God, indivisible, with liberty and justice for all."**

## ONE NATION

**THE U.S. HAS THE WORLD'S RICHEST ECONOMY** in terms of annual GDP, yet the nation is experiencing historic levels of income inequality. And even in the developing world, there are emerging concerns about whether workers will benefit from their countries' increasing prosperity. Economic inequality is the number one prevailing attribute of a Plutocratic Society. Other attributes entail low social mobility and workers struggling to climb out of poverty, governed by the socialist rich who promote self-serving Neoclassical Economic Policies of Capitalism to the poor. This describes the current U.S. and the majority of Western Civilizations today.

• Ironically, simultaneous civil unrest movements are playing out internationally and more specifically throughout all of Western Civilization where capitalism is king and European culture has dominated and oppressed its minority disenfranchised brethren for centuries through imposing multitudes of biased socioeconomic systems, laws, and policies that restrict upward mobility and diminish future aspirations.

Today, Individualism has all but disappeared in the sense that it existed during the conception of America. Individualism today offers no validation of self-worth or recognition of achievement. Instead, it celebrates selfishness and fear of change. Most Americans have become conformists. Trapped in the pursuit of short-term happiness and gratification, we are willing to endure corruption, degradation, and disenfranchisement at the hands of the Corporations we helped raise to power; corporations whose economic influence decides the culture and morals of its citizens. Our lack of a sense of common purpose and concern for the common good, works against the true meaning of democracy. We are so busy chasing that darn *"Golden Rabbit,"* we turn a blind eye to the socioeconomic systems that continue to DIVIDE and ENSLAVE us.

Most White Americans', are born with middle class economic advantages that automatically increases their opportunities to succeed and lead productive lives, while most minorities are born with far less means that definitely lessens their probabilities for success.

Current U.S. socioeconomic policy/systems make it IMPOSSIBLE to even remotely consider itself as being ONE NATION.

## Today the U.S. is FourNations:

- *Economically: Separate and Unequal*

- *Classically: The Elite (1% ) and the Rest (99%)*

## UNDER GOD:

Although the U.S. professed to be founded on religious principles, she has gradually denounced and defiled those principles steadily throughout her turbulent history. So much so, America is now deemed a SECULAR NATION.

- *Without Christ – Societies historically have always degenerated and eventually experience greater and greater social turmoil.*

**Insight**: Throughout the history of the world, God has exacted his wrath against many nations that were thought to be the most powerful nations of their time, completely destroying them as a result of their sinful and defiling humanistic .

During the horrific Blood Diamond conflict throughout the African Nations of Sierra Leone, Liberia, Ivory Coast, and the Congo, one of the "*Top native South African Traders*" after living and witnessing the destructive forces of Apartheid and now the inhumane practices of the Diamond trade declared,

"God left Africa a long time ago."

The same can be said for America today,

"*There was a Balm in Gilead*" i.e. America that also left long ago (Jeremiah 8:22).

- *God* does not dwell in defiled places. He comes and blesses a few righteous souls, then moves on to places where there exist more spiritual children.

## Religion

Most Believers only worship one God, but idolize and serve many transitory gods — such as self, money, cars, houses, celebrities, sex, drugs alcohol, pets etc.— both purposefully and unconsciously.

Jesus humbled himself by becoming obedient until death (Philippians 2:8).

Selfishness and superiority can divide people, but humility unites us into being one spirit and mind; we have to learn to value others above ourselves.

Currently, there is a so called "Ecumenical Movement" promoting unity among the World's Christian Churches, but will it have a positive impact?

"There will come one day a personal and direct touch from God, when every tear and perplexity – every oppression – every suffering and pain – wrong and distress and injustice will have a complete, ample, and overwhelming explanation" (Oswald Chambers).

Surely, we have more than fifty righteous amongst us (Genesis 18:26).

# INDIVISIBLE:

According to a resounding confirmation article posted in *Nation of Change* (Op-Ed), on December 14, 2015, by Paul Buchheit entitled, *"Half of Your Country is In-or-Near-Poverty."*

Recent reports have documented and further confirmed my position of the growing rates of impoverishment in the U.S. New information surfacing in the past twelve months shows that the trend is continuing, and worsening.

"Congress should be filled with guilt and shame for failing to deal with the enormous wealth disparities that are turning our country into the equivalent of a third world nation."

## *Half of Americans Make Less than a Living Wage*
According to the Obama Administration, over half of Americans make less than $30,000 per year.

That's less than an appropriate average living wage of $16.87 per hour as calculated by Alliance (AJS). And, it's not enough — *even with two full-time workers*— to attain an adequate but modest standard of living for a *family of four*, which at the median is over $60,000 according to the Economic Policy Institute.

AJS also found that there are *seven job seekers for every job opening* that pays enough ($15/hr.) for a single adult to make ends meet.

## *Half of Americans Have No Savings*

A study by Go Banking Rates reveals that nearly 50% of Americans have no savings. Over 70% of us have less than $1,000. Pew Research supports this finding with survey results that show nearly half of American households spending more than they earn. The lack of savings is particularly evident with young adults, who went from a 5% savings rate before the recession to a *negative savings rate* today.

## *Nearly Two-Thirds of Americans Can't Afford to Fix Their Cars*

The *Wall Street Journal* reported on a Bank rate study, which found 62 percent of Americans without the available funds for a $500 brake job. A Federal Reserve survey found that nearly half of respondents could not cover a $400 emergency expense.

It's continually getting worse, even at upper middle class levels. The *Journal* recently reported on a JP Morgan study's conclusion that the bottom 80% of households by income lack sufficient savings to cover the type of volatility observed in income and spending.

## *The Middle Class Is Disappearing*

This chart from The Huffington Post shows the dramatic shrinking of the middle class, defined as adults whose annual household income is two-thirds to double the national median, about $42,000 to $126,000 annually in 2014 dollars.

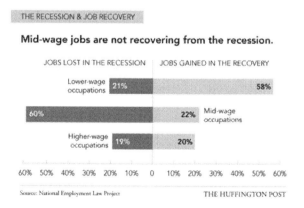

THE RECESSION & JOB RECOVERY

**Mid-wage jobs are not recovering from the recession.**

JOBS LOST IN THE RECESSION | JOBS GAINED IN THE RECOVERY

Lower-wage occupations 21% — 58%

Mid-wage occupations 60% — 22%

Higher-wage occupations 19% — 20%

Source: National Employment Law Project          THE HUFFINGTON POST

Market watchers rave about 'strong' and even 'blockbuster' job reports. But, any upbeat news about the unemployment rate should be balanced against the fact that nine of the ten fastest growing occupations don't require a college degree. Jobs *gained* since the recession, are paying *23% less* than jobs lost. Low-wage jobs (under $14 per hour) made up just 1/5 of the jobs lost to the recession, but accounted for nearly 3/5 of the jobs regained in the first three years of the recovery.

When the incomes of the Majority Working Class declines and begins to collapse, a form of debasement occurs; the value, quality, or reputation of someone or something is lowered.

Furthermore, the official 5% unemployment rate is nearly 10% when short-term discouraged workers are included and 23% when long-term discouraged workers are included. People are falling fast from the ranks of middle-class living. Between 2007 and 2013, median wealth dropped a shocking 40%, leaving the poorest half with debt-driven negative wealth.

Members of Congress comfortably nestled in bed with millionaire friends and corporate lobbyists are delusional about the true state of the American middle class. The once vibrant middle of America has dropped to lower middle, and it is still falling.

### Cultural Collective Delusion

America, it is now time to cast aside all of our xenophobic delusion and challenge ourselves collectively. For waiting on our government, corporate, and religious leaders to initiate effective political, economic, and moral change has clearly been undeniably proven to not be realistic. Therefore, we must recognize that "no one is invisible." Everyone deserves to be seen.If you want to make this once great Nation of ours' a better place, look at yourself in the mirror, and become the change you seek.

- "I am a Man of Substance, of flesh and bone, fiber and liquids – and might even be said to possess a Mind…I am Invisible, understand, simply because People Refuse to See Me." (Ralph Ellison).

*"Oftentimes, we're all guilty of looking past others yet never seeing them."*

**Based on the current socioeconomic conditions existent in the U.S. today, our Founding Fathers would be rolling over in their graves and here's why:**

- America today is more divided than at any other time in its history.
- America today functions and operates outside the protection of God's Laws.
- Liberty and Justice for all has no application in American Society today.
- In 2018, 51% 0f all school age children in America will be minorities.
- 56% of all U.S. Schools are classified as Title I; whereby at least 40% of total students are in poverty.
- 110 million Americans are working poor; 15.5 million children live in poverty; U.S. poverty has increased 246% from 1935 – 2013.
- 51% of the total Federal Budget is spent on entitlement programs.
- 52.1% of U.S. High School Students never attend College
- America is the only free-market OECD Country – where the current generation is less educated than the previous one.
- 62.6% U.S. National Labor Participation Rate is the lowest since 1978.
- 77% of all U.S. Public Schools are segregated – Same as 1968.
- 32 million U.S. citizens are illiterate;19% of all U.S. High School graduates can't read.
- 49 million U.S. citizens are food insecure; 15.8 million are children.
- 2.2 million U.S. Prisoners (80% Minorities): total population is highest per-capita worldwide.
- 2.5 million U.S. youth are homeless; (Government documented… more undocumented).
- $7.25/hr. minimum wage has the same purchasing power as 1968; adjusted for inflation.
- 3.65 million baby- boomers per year are retiring for the next 19 years; 76 million jobs will be eliminated.
- $18.92 trillion U.S. National Debt versus $18.06 GDP; U.S. Debt to GDP Ratio 105 % (second highest in U.S. history) and has increased 3,807% from 1995 – 2015); the highest being the "Great Depression" of 1946 (121.70%).

- 20% of the entire U.S. Budget is spent on defense and security (Debt increased $640 billion from 2014 – 2015) – U.S. remains in a financial crisis.
- $2.1 Trillion Corporate Inversion profit parked in U.S. Banks – (untouchable tax free); the average American family pays more in income taxes in one year than dozens of these respective tax dodging corporation's pay in five years.
- The U.S. is bankrupt, yet Wall Street capitalists are experiencing record profits.
- The U.S. fiat capitalistic system is unsustainable. You can't have an effective economic system where fewer and fewer people participate - U.S. Capitalism is destroying itself.
- 50% of the U.S. population earns less than $30,000 per year.
- The average American is indebted $21,700 per year to support government entitlements.
- It costs the average American $31,000 per year to house the nations' prisoners.
- Every American citizen is indebted to the Government $154,161 to cover the national debt.
- The Social Security Trust Fund lost $3 billion in 2015 for the first time since 1983 and since 2010, pays out more than it collects - without reform, it will become insolvent by 2029.

*"The cross doesn't discriminate."*

# Epilogue

**America – waiting on the other side of "xenophobic delusion" is your destiny.**

*Based on the indisputable Truths put forth before you;*

1.  Do you think Social Security can survive with less labor force participation (62.6%)?

2.  Do you think Medicare expenses will continue to increase while offering less coverage?

3.  Do you think Individual Retirement Accounts are secure from the Government; MyRA and Capital Controls... Bail-In tactics made legal?

4.  Do you think taxes will go up or down in future years?

5.  How long do you think the Government can afford to spend 51% of its budget on social welfare?

6.  How long do you think the Government can continue to print Fiat Money, sell worthless Bonds, and continue to borrow against the future production of its declining workforce?

7.  How long do you think the Government can continue to spend 20% of its Budget on Defense?

8.  Do you believe the Government is currently bankrupt?

9.  Do you believe the Baby boomer generation has squandered the future inheritance of the next three generations?

10. Do you believe the Government is in control of our economy or Wall Street Capitalist?

11. Do you believe that another "National Financial Crisis" is near?

12. Do you believe a new President regardless of Race, Gender, Party will be for the People, or just another "Musical Chairman"?

13. Do you believe the current $21,700/year you support for Government social welfare will continue to increase or decline?

14. Do you believe the U.S. prison population will continue to increase or decrease and that your financial obligation of $31,000 per year, per inmate, will follow suit respectively?

15. How do you think any of us will be able to afford to pay the Government $154,161 to help satisfy the national debt in our lifetimes - through taxation, labor, forfeiture or otherwise?

16. Do you believe any of us will be able to afford to retire with only 48% of all eligible U.S. High School students attending College; while 70% of all future jobs will require a minimum two year college degree?

17. Do you believe your Social Security will be available when you retire, with less people working, less students attending College, and with the Governments' continued borrowing?

## *The Economic Advantages of Cultural Unity*

Altarum Institute in 2015, studied the effect of closing the minority earnings gap in the U.S and found that if the average incomes of minorities were raised to the average incomes of Whites, total U.S. earnings would increase by 12%, representing nearly $1 trillion today. By closing the earnings gap through higher productivity, gross domestic product would increase by a comparable percentage, for an increase of $1.9 trillion today. The earnings gain would translate into $180 billion in additional corporate profits, $290 billion in additional federal tax revenues, and a potential reduction in the federal deficit of $350 billion, or 2.3% of the GDP. When projected to 2030 and 2050, the results are even more startling. Minorities make up 37% of the working age population now, but they are projected to grow to 46% by 2030, and 55% by 2050. Closing the earnings gap by 2030 would increase the GDP by 16%, or more than $5 trillion a year. Federal tax revenues would increase by over $1 trillion and corporate profits would increase by $450 billion. By 2050, closing the gap would increase GDP by 20%. This is roughly the size of the entire federal budget, and a higher percentage than all U.S. healthcare expenditures! In addition, national debt would be reduced due to less minorities being dependent on current Federal Supplemental Entitlement Assistance.

- A 2014 U.S. Department of Commerce study estimated that if income inequalities were eliminated, minority purchasing power would increase from a baseline projection of $4.3 trillion in 2045 to $6.1 trillion (in 1998 dollars), accounting for 70% of all U.S. purchases!

## *Where Much is Sacrificed, Much is Gained*

Approximately 50% of the total U.S. Population (160 Million People) are in or near poverty; earning income of less than $30,000 per year. If you are fortunate enough to not be one of them, be compassionate enough to help one of them. As believers in Christ, it's our moral duty to help others beyond ourselves.

- *To put this in a clearer perspective; if we raised the minimum wage to $15.00 per hour (equates to $30,600 per year) – the net effect on the 160 million people cited above would be unchanged.*

This is truly the greatest human atrocity of our time…"*Our fears reveal our hearts intent.*"

- As believers, we should all strive to get rich in the gospel versus wordly passions.

- In a Progressive Society, in order to meet our common economic, social, and cultural needs, we must first liberate ourselves from Globalization, and start yielding benefits from a communal sense of fellowship, responsibility, and purpose in life driven by production versus consumption.

Believers must learn to humble themselves by learning to forgive and forget.

Many Believers can learn and grow spiritually to forgive but forgetting is the bigger challenge.

Many believe in order to forget means to not learn from the experience so they hold on to it.

So, how do we learn to forget? We need to change our limited understanding and change our perspective spiritually. To forget does not mean to literally erase something from our memory. For as humans, we are incapable of doing so. Spiritually, it means to not harbor hatred and malice in your heart by eliminating all grudges and ill feeling towards others, reconciling our differences through practicing reciprocity.

A change of heart is the beginning of reconciliation

- If the Lord delivered dominion to mankind through his son Jesus Christ, why have so many refused to accept Him?

- How can we begin to create cultural unity if we refuse to show humility in openly welcoming and accepting one another in Christ?

Therefore, go and make disciples of all Nations (Matthew 28:19).

Insight: Nation is derived from the Greek word Ethos which is also the source of the word Ethnic.

Therefore, this means, go and make disciples of all ethnicities, i.e. "Unity in the Body of Christ."

## *Develop an Altruistic Spirit*

Achieving racial equity requires eliminating racial barriers in opportunities and outcomes for all people. Racial equity is a socioeconomic necessity. By helping to build the capabilities of those who are the furthest behind, we not only begin to solve our most serious challenge, we also create the conditions that allow us all to prosper. **The only solution is cultural unity** which can only be created through true heart based "***Socal Stewardship***" (LifeWorkz Global, Inc. – www. lifeworkzglo.org).

## *BEST National Investment Strategy:*

- The absolute safest and highest yielding investment available today resides in us collectively strengthening and serving one another. This guarantees the maximum return on investment (ROI).

Either we'll learn to live righteously together or dig our own graves.

***Stop chasing that darn silly Rabbit and start chasing God.***

## *CHASING GOD – SERVING MAN*

The key is for God's people to cross the dividing lines of passion and compassion and meet Him at the convergence of the cross; "where passion and compassion.intersect." God always comes to us in the middle where two or three are gathered together in His Presence (Matt 18:20). Building a House of Bethany…a Bethany Nation – " ***BEYOND XENOPHOBIA.***"

> *"THERE IS POWER IN THE NAME OF JESUS TO BREAK EVERY CHAIN."*

Step into a New World – A New Life Outside - Serving Others… (LifeWorkz Global, Inc. – www.lifeworkzglo.org).

# Sources

1. "We have just enough religion to make us hate, but not enough to make us love one another" (Jonathan Swift).

2. "For if any be a hearer of the Word, and not a doer, he is like unto a man beholding his natural face in a mirror" (James 1:23).

3. *"Set your mind on things that are above, not on things that are on earth"* (Colossians3:2).

4. James Baldwin - Root.com as quoted from Ebony Magazine 11/27/15

5. "There's a great invisible strength in a peoples union." - President Lincoln

6. Brooking Report Study 2015, *OPPORTUNITY, RESPONSIBILITY, and SECURITY: A CONSENSUS PLAN FOR REDUCING POVERTY AND RESTORING THE AMERICAN DREAM:*

7. "There is neither Jew nor Greek nor slave nor free for we are all one in Jesus Christ Lord of all." (Galatians 3:28).

8. "Every kingdom divided against itself will be laid waste, and every city or household divided against itself will not stand." *(Matthew 12:25).*

9. *Chasing God, Serving Man (Tommy Tenney)*

10. *"Unjust Laws are like no Laws at all." (St. Augustine)*

11. *Bethany: The House of revival (evanwiggs.com)*

12. "It does not belong to man…to direct his step" (Jcremiah 10:23)

13. November 9, 2015, *Atlanta Journal Constitution (AJC)*Article – "Get Schooled" by Maureen Downey

14. *Think Progress*, by Alan Pyke on December 2, 2015, there has been 355 mass shootings this year in the United States, more than one for every day of the year so far.

15. *Think Progress* on December 2, 2015, by Alex Zielinski disclosed the far-reaching influence the NRA has not only in Washington, but on the entire Medical Industry alike.

16. CNN Special Report – Race and Reality in America by Catherine E. Shoichet**, posted** on November 25, 2015

17. White America's Greatest Delusion: "They do not know it and They Do Not Want to Know It" – "*It is the innocence which constitutes the crime" (James Baldwin.)*

18. "**Whoever says he is in the light and hates his brother** is still in darkness" (1 John 2:9).

19. "I have a dream that my four little children will one day live in a nation where they will not be judged by the color of their skin**, but by the content of their characte**r" (Dr. Martin Luther King, Jr.).

20. "When we let freedom ring, when we let it ring from every village and every hamlet, from every state and every city, we will be able to speed up that day when all of God's children, Black men and White men, Jews and Gentiles, Protestants and Catholics, will be able to join hands and sing in the words of the old Negro spiritual, **Free at Last! Free at Last! Thank God Almighty, we are Free at Last!**" (Dr. Martin Luther King, Jr.)

21. Conventional Cultural Unity; openDemocracy.net, February 29, 2012

22. UN Chronicle (Unity in Diversity), September 2012

23. "God's Plan and Purpose for Christ was to Unite All Things in Heaven and on Earth."(Ephesians 1:9-10)

24. July/August 2015 publication of Fast Company, Assistant Editor Austin Carr disclosed details of his exclusive interview with Starbucks CEO Howard Schultz regarding their recently launched controversial Race Together Campaign in late March 2015.

25. Hayley Peterson of Yahoo Finance on December 14, 2015, Sam's Club CEO Rosalind Brewer

26. God revealed his plan and purpose for Christ – "To bring unity to all things in heaven and on earth (Ephesians 1:9 – 10 NIV).

27. *Future Work*- Fear of the Outlander (Tom Payne)

28. Four Horsemen Documentary 2012

29. Richard Adams of *The Guardian* captured the following quote by **Lloyd Blankfein, CEO of Goldman Sachs (GS),** providing the following justifications for their firm's obvious unethical practices when questioned by the U.S. Senate on April 27, 2009:

30. *New York Times* article by Gretchen Morgenson and Don Van Natta, Jr. on August 8, 2009 – The Financial Crisis.

31. *Huffington Post* on November 16, 2015, by Zach Carter, Senior Political Economy Reporter, in WASHINGTON, DC, House Republicans on Monday unveiled legislation that would decriminalize a broad swath of corporate malfeasance

32. ***"People will even Abandon Their Religion if it conflicts with Their Economic Interests"***-Samuel Eliot Morison

33. "My Kingdom was not part of this world" (John 18:36 KJV).

34. CNN report on December 8, 2015, a San Bernardino Muslim terrorist attack left fourteen dead

35. December 8, 2015, *New York Times* article by Elizabeth Dias - Donald Trump's Muslim ban rallies religious leaders against him.

36. *Nation of Change* on November 22, 2015, by Michael Payne: "*Where American Socialism and Capitalism Blend Together Perfectly*"

37. "But for those who are self-seeking and reject the truth and follow evil, there will be wrath and anger" (Romans 2:8 NIV).

38. "He who controls the Past – controls the Future" *(George Orwell)*.

39. According to a July 28, 2014, article published by *Philosophical Economics* - Two Misconceptions about the Gold Standard.

40. *New Economic Perspective* on January 2, 2013, by Devin Smith who referenced excerpts from the very respected works of Pulitzer Prize winner, Edward O. Wilson's book, *The Social Conquest of Earth*. The book takes an in-depth look at what happens when a Sovereign Power becomes a Democracy?

41. According to an insightful article in *Forbes* on October 28, 2014, by Mike Patton - Owners of U.S. Debt.

42. U.S. Treasury Department 2014

43. According to James Dale Davidson (Well endowed Economist) May 2016 Article – *2016 Economic Collapse/Elimination of Social Security*

44. *TEA PARTY.org* article published on February 14, 2014, "Obamanomics."

45. Forecasts & Trends E-Letter by Gary D. Halbert, published on May 6, 2014, ***Are Currency Controls also known as Capital Controls Coming to America July 1, 2014?***

46. Urban Institute 2015 report – The Naked truth

47. U.C. Berkeley study published in 2015 on Minimum Wages

48. *Mic.com* by Eviya Iranovska on March 26, 2012

49. Sociologist Robert Bellah and his coauthors first published their gut-checking book, *Creating the Good Society* in 1991; it became a wake-up call and rallying cry for America.

50. *Nation of Change* on January 11, 2016, by Paul Buchheit, *"The Real Terrorists: The .01%"*

51. "Think of your brethren like unto yourselves, and be familiar with all and free with your substance, that they may be rich like unto you" (Jacob 2:17).

52. "There is **no future for mankind** unless tolerance and understanding between cultures and nations become the rule instead of the exception" (UN Secretary General Kurt Waldheim 2012).

53. *The U.S. News and World Report – "The Conversation" on December 14, 2015*

54. The Civil Rights Project on September 19, 2012, Guy Orfield

55. Nicole Hannah-Jones article, Segregation Now – 2014 Study conducted by Rucker Johnson, a public-policy professor at the University of California at Berkeley, published by the National Bureau of Economic Research.

56. The Center for American Progress, an independent bipartisan educational institute, released a report in August 2015

57. *Washington Post* article- Students in Poverty, July 2, 2012

58. *AJC* Education Report, January 7, 2016

59. "Many Students give correct answers on tests, but fail to put those lessons into practice – Undigested Knowledge"(Lancelot Oliphant).

60. 2013 National Assessment of Education Program (NAEP)

61. *New York Times* article on Schools with High Poverty, published January 16, 2015

62. The U.S. President's Council on Jobs and Economic Competitiveness

63. Center on Budget and Policy Priorities (CBPP) 2014

64. September 2015 *Atlanta Journal Constitution (AJC)* report, by 2020, 60% of all Georgia jobs will require Post-Secondary Education

65. August 2015 Georgia Budget and Policy Report

66. October 26, 2015 report *"Jim Crow now Juan Crow in Georgia"* by Angela D. Meltzer (*AJC*)

67. AJC (In-State Tuition Waivers) Janel Davis, March 18, 2015

68. The National Coalition for the Homeless Study – November 2014

69. *Huffington Post* College Article posted on August 26, 2011, "Freedom University

70. *Alternet* article, "21st Century Slaves: How Corporations Exploit Prison Labor," published July 11, 2011

71. The *Atlantic* "Prison Labor in America", published September 21, 2015

72. *Left Business Observer* 2015 Report

73. National Institute of Justice Report dated June 17, 2014

74. *Take Part Organization Immigration Labor* article in 2014

75. President Obama's (Immigration Executive Actions) November 2014

76. "After Him, the Priests, the men of the Valley, carried out repairs" (Nehemiah 3:22 NASB).

77. *Hearts That We Broke Long Ago* (Merele Shaine)

78. U.S. Department of Education Report 2013

79. *Urban Diversity* May 1, 2015, by Nate Silver

80. *Bloomberg Business News* article published on May 4, 2015 – U.S. companies are stashing $2.1 trillion overseas to avoid taxes

81. *Wall Street Journal - "Firms Keep Stockpiles of 'Foreign' Cash in U.S."* by KATE LINEBAUGH Jan. 22, 2013

82. "And being found in fashion as a man, he humbled himself, and became obedient unto death, even the death of the cross" (Philippians 2:8 KJV).

83. "There will come one day a personal and direct touch from God, when every tear and perplexity – every oppression – every suffering and pain –wrong and distress and injustice will have a complete, ample, and overwhelming explanation" (Oswald Chambers).

84. "And the Lord said, If I find in Sodom fifty righteous within the city, then I will spare all the place for their sakes" (Genesis 18:26).

85. Is there no balm in Gilead; is there no physician there? Why then is not the health of the daughter of my people recovered? (Jeremiah 8:22 KJV).

86. *Nation of Change* (Op-Ed), on December 14, 2015, by Paul Buchheit entitled, *"Half of Your Country is In-or-Near-Poverty."*

87. I am a Man of Substance, of flesh and bone, fiber and liquids – and might even be said to possess a Mind...I am Invisible, understand, simply because People Refuse to See Me." (Ralph Ellison).

88. Altarum Institute in 2015, studied the effect of closing the minority earnings gap in the U.S

89. "Therefore go and make disciples of all nations, baptizing them in the name of the Father and of the Son and of the Holy Spirit" (Matthew 28:19 NIV).

90. For where two or three are gathered together in my name, there am I in the midst of them" (Matthew 18:20).

Made in the USA
Columbia, SC
09 June 2020